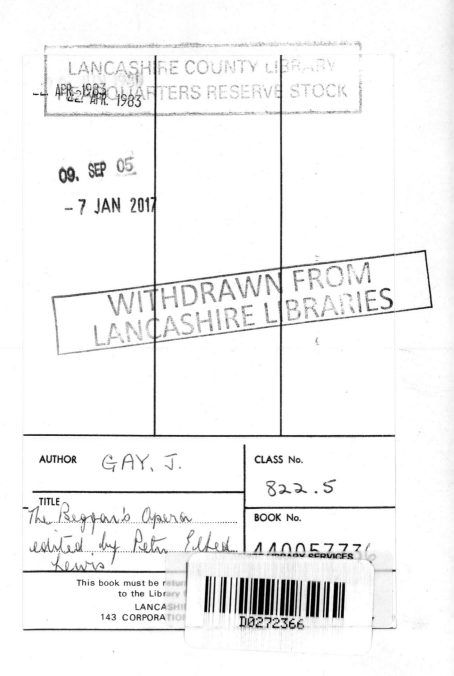

AUTHOR   GAY, J.

CLASS No.

822.5

TITLE

The Beggar's Opera

edited by Peter Elbert

Lewis

BOOK No.

440057773

THE BEGGAR'S OPERA

JOHN GAY

THE BEGGAR'S OPERA

Edited by
PETER ELFED LEWIS

Nos haec novimus esse nihil.   Martial

OLIVER & BOYD
EDINBURGH
1973

OLIVER AND BOYD
Croythorn House
23 Ravelston Terrace
Edinburgh EH4 3TJ
(A Division of Longman Group Limited)

First published 1973

0 05 002717 4 Hardback
0 05 002716 6 Paperback

440057736

Printed in Great Britain by
Cox & Wyman Ltd
London, Fakenham and Reading

CONTENTS

ACKNOWLEDGMENTS

This edition is the culmination of my research into the plays of John Gay, which was begun in 1962 when I was a postgraduate student at the University of Leeds, working on the satirical and burlesque drama of the early eighteenth century under the supervision of the late Professor Douglas Grant. I would like to take this opportunity to acknowledge my indebtedness to him. I would also like to thank two other members of the School of English at Leeds who helped me considerably: Professor A. Norman Jeffares, who suggested that I prepare this edition, encouraged me to do so, and kindly read the final draft; and John Horden, Director of the Institute of Bibliography and Textual Criticism, whose assistance during the later stages, especially regarding textual matters, was painstaking and invaluable. I am extremely grateful to Professor Vinton A. Dearing of the University of California for providing me with the results of his own bibliographical research into the play when I was working on the final revisions last year. I have been able to incorporate references to his work in my Introduction. In addition to the many librarians in numerous libraries, both English and American, who assisted me, I would like to thank the following: Professor Frank Dowrick of the Faculty of Law of Durham University who helped me to explicate some of the legal allusions and references in the play; Miss Jessie Dobson, Curator of the Hunterian Museum at the Royal College of Surgeons, who provided me with the historical information relating to the Barber-Surgeons' Hall; the Research Fund Committee of Durham University for their generous financial assistance without which this edition would not have been possible; Nanette Clayton who patiently typed and retyped much of the manuscript; and Tony Seward of Oliver and Boyd for his great help in preparing this edition for the press. The reproduction of the first leaf of the First Edition (title-page on the recto and Dramatis Personae on the verso), which is included in order to give some idea of the typographical appearance of the edition on which mine is based, was made from the copy in the Brotherton Collection, Brotherton Library, Leeds University by kind permission of the University Librarian and Keeper of the Collection, Mr D. Cox.

Durham   PETER ELFED LEWIS
August 1972

A CHRONOLOGY OF THE PRINCIPAL WORKS
OF JOHN GAY (1685–1732)

1708   *Wine*, a long poem, published anonymously.

1711   *The Present State of Wit*, an essay, published.

1712   *The Mohocks*, a 'Tragi-Comical Farce', published but not performed.

1713   *Rural Sports*, a long poem, published.
        The Wife of Bath, a comedy with 'Characters from *Chaucer's* Days', produced at Drury Lane and published.
        The Fan, a long poem, published.

1714   *The Shepherd's Week*, a sequence of pastoral poems, published.

1715   *The What D'Ye Call It*, a 'Tragi-Comi-Pastoral Farce', produced at Drury Lane and published.

1716   *Trivia; or, The Art of Walking the Streets of London*, a long poem, published.

1717   *Three Hours after Marriage*, a comedy written in collaboration with Pope and Arbuthnot, produced at Drury Lane and published.

1719   *Acis and Galatea*, an 'English Pastoral Opera' by Handel with a libretto by Gay, privately performed at Canons, the seat of the Duke of Chandos.

1720   *Poems on Several Occasions* published. This contains much of Gay's work up to this date, including the unperformed and previously unpublished 'Pastoral Tragedy', *Dione*.

1724   *The Captives*, a tragedy, produced at Drury Lane and published.

1727   *Fables* (First Series) published.

1728   *The Beggar's Opera* produced at Lincoln's Inn Fields and published.

1729   *Polly*, the sequel to *The Beggar's Opera*, published after the production being arranged was banned by the Government in December 1728.

1730   A radically revised version of *The Wife of Bath* produced at Lincoln's Inn Fields and published.

1732   The text of *Acis and Galatea* published. The first public performance took place at Lincoln's Inn Fields in 1731.

1733   *Achilles*, a ballad opera, produced at Covent Garden and published.

1734   *The Distress'd Wife*, a comedy, produced at Covent Garden.

1738 *Fables* (Second Series) published.
1743 *The Distress'd Wife* published.
1754 *The Rehearsal at Goatham*, an unperformed comedy, published.
1777 *Polly* produced for the first time, at the Theatre Royal in the Haymarket.

INTRODUCTION

I. THE PLAY

John Gay (1685–1732), who came from an old Devonshire family and who was born and educated in Barnstaple, is one of the most important Augustan writers, though not of the stature of his close friends Pope and Swift. *The Beggar's Opera* is Gay's greatest work and one of the masterpieces of Augustan literature. It is also one of the very few eighteenth century plays that have survived in the theatre to become classics of English drama. In spite of the topical nature of much of its social and political satire, not to mention its burlesque of Italian opera, *The Beggar's Opera* successfully transcends its period. One of the greatest dramatists of the twentieth century, Bertolt Brecht, found inspiration in the play, and in his brilliant modernisation of it, *Die Dreigroschenoper* or *The Threepenny Opera* (1928), he adapted Gay's irony to express his Marxist view that the criminal and the capitalist are essentially identical. From Gay's highly original use of popular music, Brecht also learned how to create a drama that would be both entertaining and intellectual, appeal to a mass audience and yet be an instrument of social change.[1] After nearly two and a half centuries *The Beggar's Opera* is as alive as it ever was. It is exceedingly ironic that the play should bear the epigraph, *'Nos haec novimus esse nihil'* ('We know these things to be nothing'), taken from Martial (*Epigrammata*, XIII, 2—'In Detractorem').

The origin of *The Beggar's Opera* is usually believed to be Swift's suggestion, made in a letter to Pope dated 30 August 1716, that Gay should write 'a Newgate pastoral, among the whores and thieves there',[2] but Gay did not write the play until 1727 when he and Swift were staying at Pope's house in Twickenham. More immediate sources of inspiration were the criminal careers of Jack Sheppard, executed in 1724, and especially

[1] For a comparison of Gay and Brecht, see J. J. Sherwin, '"The World is Mean and Man Uncouth"', in *Virginia Quarterly Review*, XXXV (1959), pp. 258–70.

[2] *The Correspondence of Jonathan Swift*, ed. H. Williams (Oxford, 1963), vol. II, p. 215.

of Jonathan Wild, executed in 1725, both of whom are discussed later.[3] Although his two friends certainly encouraged Gay to work on the play, neither Pope nor Swift contributed much more than advice. It is not impossible that Pope amended a couple of lines in Air I or even that he provided Air LXVII as William Ayre claims,[4] but the once widely-held view that Pope added most of the satire against the Court and the Government is completely erroneous.[5] According to William Cooke,[6] Air VI was written by Sir Charles Hanbury Williams, Air XXIV by William Fortescue, Air XXX by Swift, and Air XLIV by Lord Chesterfield, but Cooke's testimony, based on that of Lady Townshend, lacks authority. *The Beggar's Opera* is almost entirely Gay's own creation, as Pope himself testifies.[7] Gay probably began writing the play in the summer of 1727 and did not take long to complete it. In a letter to Swift dated 22 October 1727 he states that his 'Opera is already finished'.[8]

Towards the end of 1727 Gay offered *The Beggar's Opera* to Colley Cibber, the manager of the Theatre Royal in Drury Lane, but he rejected it. Cibber probably felt that it would be unwise to stage a play containing such incisive satire of the Court and of the King's chief Minister of State, Sir Robert Walpole, although he also seems to have been put off by its originality and novelty. After this rejection, Gay's patroness, the Duchess of Queensbury, used her influence with John Rich, the manager of the Theatre Royal in Lincoln's Inn Fields, to persuade him to produce it. Before the play opened on 29 January 1728, some of Gay's friends, including Swift and Pope, were apprehensive about its reception. After reading the manuscript Congreve is reported to have said, 'It would either take greatly, or be damned confoundedly',[9] and Pope wrote to Swift that 'it will make a great noise, but whether of Claps or Hisses I

---

[3] For an interesting suggestion about Gay's detailed knowledge of Newgate Prison and the slang of the underworld, see James R. Sutherland's letter to *The Times Literary Supplement* listed in the Bibliography.

[4] *Memoirs of the Life and Writings of Alexander Pope, Esq.* (London, 1745), vol. II, pp. 115–6. Ayre's claim is restated by Henry Angelo in his *Reminiscences* (London, 1828), vol. I, pp. 25–6.

[5] See William Broome's letter dated 3 May 1728 to Elijah Fenton in *The Correspondence of Alexander Pope*, ed. G. Sherburn (Oxford, 1956), vol. II, p. 489. Also Ayre, *loc. cit.*, and Angelo, *loc. cit.*

[6] *Memoirs of Charles Macklin, Comedian* (London, 1804), p. 60.

[7] See J. Spence, *Observations, Anecdotes, and Characters of Books and Men*, ed. J. M. Osborn (Oxford, 1966), vol. I, p. 107.

[8] *The Letters of John Gay*, ed. C. F. Burgess (Oxford, 1966), p. 69.

[9] See Spence, *loc. cit.*

know not'.[10] On the first night the audience, which included Walpole, took a little while to accustom themselves to the radically new form of the ballad opera, but they finally received the play with enormous enthusiasm. The play did 'take greatly', and a contemporary witticism was that it made 'Rich gay and Gay rich'.

Before the end of the 1727–8 season the play was performed sixty-two times, and this almost unbelievable and unprecedented success was repeated in the next theatrical season during which fifty-nine performances were given, sixteen of them by a company of child-actors called the Lilliputians. By present standards these runs are not remarkable, but in the eighteenth century single nights were common and a run of about six performances usual. The fame of *The Beggar's Opera* spread so rapidly that it was acted in the provinces and in Dublin during its first London season, a very unusual occurrence indeed for a new play. It remained very popular throughout the eighteenth century, being performed every year after 1727, and it continued to hold the stage during the nineteenth century although performances gradually became less frequent. The main roles (Polly, Lucy, Macheath, Peachum and Lockit) and a few of the minor ones, like Mrs Peachum and Mrs Trapes, are such wonderful acting parts that they have remained a constant attraction to actors and actresses. There have been many successful revivals in the twentieth century, including Nigel Playfair's almost legendary production at the Lyric Theatre, Hammersmith, during the early Twenties with Frederic Austin's version of the music. Since then other composers, notably Benjamin Britten, have made new musical arrangements.

One reason for its initial success was the high quality of the first production. Rich assembled a very good cast, and Lavinia Fenton, who played Polly Peachum, and Thomas Walker, who played Macheath, were superb. According to some reports it was Lavinia Fenton's singing of '*Oh, ponder well! be not severe*' (Air XII towards the end of Act I) that won over the audience on the first night. Whether or not this is true, her moving performance as the very sympathetic heroine of the play did make her famous overnight and the toast of the town. But in order to understand why the play was so popular when it first appeared and why it remained so popular, it is necessary to clarify the various elements that Gay skilfully weaves together in his ballad opera.

In 1728 *The Beggar's Opera* was a daring social and political satire, and also a radically new departure in opera because of its use of popular tunes and of 'low' subject-matter. In addition it burlesqued the dominant

---

[10] *Correspondence*, ed. Sherburn, vol. II, p. 469.

operatic form of the day, Italian opera. It can also be seen as a lively and amusing comedy with unconventional characters and an unusual setting—'a Newgate pastoral, among the whores and thieves there'. At the same time it is the love story of the promiscuous but engaging rogue Macheath and the comparatively innocent and utterly devoted Polly, a love story that appeals to the emotions and at times achieves genuine pathos. Even Polly's main rival for Macheath's affections, the less naïve and more cunning Lucy Lockit, who is pregnant by him, is treated sympathetically. But if the play is in one way a low-life romance with Macheath as hero, Polly as major heroine and Lucy as minor heroine, it is also an anti-romance with Macheath as anti-hero and Polly and Lucy as anti-heroines ridiculing the sentimentality and spurious heroics of much serious contemporary drama and opera. The characters exist simultaneously at two levels, as anti-types at the burlesque level, and in their own right at the non-burlesque level. *The Beggar's Opera* is plainly a very complex work in which Gay achieves a most delicate balance between comedy and pathos, thus avoiding both cynicism and sentimentality. This complexity explains why productions of the play vary so much in tone, from near-farce at one extreme to near-tragedy at the other. Lucy Lockit, for example, is sometimes played as an entirely comic character, but she has also been played as a very pathetic character, a woman more sinned against than sinning. Gay undoubtedly intended something between these extremes. Some of the elements in the play, such as the comic-pathetic love story, are clear enough, but others, especially the operatic burlesque and the topical satire, require elucidation.

Although *The Beggar's Opera* is unique, it is not without precedent in Gay's output for the theatre. When it is viewed in relation to *The Mohocks* (1712), *The What D'Ye Call It* (1715) and *Three Hours after Marriage* (1717), it can be seen as the culmination of Gay's experiments in satirical drama and dramatic burlesque. *The Mohocks*, Gay's first play, degenerates into unmitigated farce, but in the fine opening scene, which burlesques both *Paradise Lost* and contemporary tragedy, the presentation of the criminal gang as a courtly assembly, with its own emperor, protocol, and standards of conduct, certainly foreshadows the ironic inversions in *The Beggar's Opera*.[11] The traces of social and political satire in *The What D'Ye Call It* are very much subservient to the excellent burlesque of contemporary tragedy, but Gay's burlesque method of uncompromising

[11] See T. B. Stroup, 'Gay's *Mohocks* and Milton', in *Journal of English and German Philology*, XLVI (1947), pp. 164–7. Also my 'Another Look at John Gay's *The Mohocks*', in *Modern Language Review*, LXIII (1968), pp. 790–3.

irony again points forward to *The Beggar's Opera*.[12] In the more crudely
farcical *Three Hours after Marriage*, written in collaboration with Pope
and John Arbuthnot (who, like Gay and Swift, were members of the
distinguished literary group known as the Scriblerus Club),[13] there is a
not wholly successful attempt to unite burlesque of farcical intrigue
comedies, ridicule of certain well-known personalities, and typically
Scriblerian satire of misdirected intellectual energy.[14] In *The Beggar's
Opera*, on the other hand, Gay does manage to integrate such disparate
elements as dramatic burlesque (mainly of Italian opera), social and
political satire, and attacks on individuals (chiefly Walpole) by reverting
to the subtler, ironic method of *The What D'Ye Call It*. Gay's use of the
'mask' or persona of the Beggar as author of the 'opera', for example,
recalls his adoption of the 'mask' of a typical contemporary dramatist in
the Preface to *The What D'Ye Call It* who presents this 'Tragi-Comi-
Pastoral Farce' as an extremely serious play. *The Beggar's Opera* is not,
therefore, a social and political satire with an added flavouring of burlesque, nor is it a dramatic burlesque with a substantial infusion of social
and political satire. It is an original imaginative conception in which
burlesque and satire are inextricably fused.

Although the passage of time has not diminished the force of Gay's
social and political satire, it has made the burlesque of Italian opera almost
incomprehensible except to students of eighteenth century culture. But if
Gay had not been intent on attacking Italian opera, he would not have
revitalised English opera by devising the new form of the ballad

---

[12] See my 'Gay's Burlesque Method in *The What D'Ye Call It*', in *Durham University Journal*, XXIX (1967–8), pp. 13–25.

[13] The other members were Thomas Parnell and Robert Harley, Earl of Oxford.
The aim of the Scriblerus Club was to satirise contemporary scientific, philosophical
and artistic follies through the fictional character of Martinus Scriblerus. For a detailed
account of the Club, see Charles Kerby-Miller's Preface to his edition of the *Memoirs
of the Extraordinary Life, Works, and Discoveries of Martinus Scriblerus* (New Haven,
1950), pp. 1-77. It is worth noting that three of the greatest works by members of the
Club, Swift's *Gulliver's Travels* (1726), Gay's *The Beggar's Opera* (1728) and Pope's
The Dunciad (first version, 1728), appeared within two years of each other.

[14] See D. F. Smith, *Plays about the Theatre in England from The Rehearsal in 1671
to the Licensing Act in 1737* (London and New York, 1936), pp. 101–8. Also *Three
Hours after Marriage*, ed. R. Morton and W. M. Peterson (Painesville, Ohio, 1961).
And my 'Dramatic Burlesque in *Three Hours after Marriage*', in *Durham University
Journal*, XXXIII (1971–2), pp. 232–9.

opera. English dramatic opera had held the stage from 1656, when Davenant's *The Siege of Rhodes* appeared, until the end of the seventeenth century, but with the premature death of Henry Purcell in 1695 it lost its one composer of genius. In the early eighteenth century it succumbed to Italian opera. The most important difference between the two forms is that Restoration dramatic opera contains comparatively little singing and consists mainly of dialogue, whereas all the words are set to music in Italian opera.[15]

A complete opera of the Italian type, *Arsinoe*, was first presented in England in 1705. The popularity of Italian opera increased rapidly, and following Handel's arrival in London in 1710 it became one of the reigning theatrical fashions. In 1720, with the support of Royalty and members of the aristocracy, Handel and his Swiss associate, John James Heidegger, founded the Royal Academy of Music in order to put Italian opera on a permanent basis in England. Yet in spite of its great success, Italian opera did not go uncriticised. Most of the criticism was in journals and periodicals like *The Spectator*, but some was embodied in dramatic burlesques and satirical plays. Richard Estcourt's *Prunella*, a nondescript burlesque aimed specifically at *Arsinoe* and *Camilla* (1706), was produced as early as 1708. A much finer burlesque is Richard Leveridge's *The Comick Masque of Pyramus and Thisbe* (1716), which is also more effective than Mrs Aubert's better-known *Harlequin-Hydaspes: or, The Greshamite* (1719), a burlesque of Mancini's *Hydaspes* (1710). The anonymous *The Contre Temps; or, Rival Queans* (1727) is directed more against the leading personages of Italian opera in London than against the form itself, but its satire is very incisive indeed.[16]

The two main reasons for the opposition to Italian opera were national prejudice and a concern for dramatic standards, the first of which was probably the more important although it is usually difficult to separate the two. Addison, for instance, regarded Italian opera as a foreign imposition on native soil, and in *The Spectator* No. 18 (21 March 1711) he

[15] In *The Beggar's Opera: Its Predecessors and Successors* (Cambridge, 1922), pp. 29–33, Frank Kidson argues as other scholars have done that Allan Ramsay's *The Gentle Shepherd* (1725) was the first ballad opera and that Gay was influenced by this pastoral play. This view is incorrect, as Burns Martin in *Allan Ramsay: A Study of his Life and Works* (Cambridge, Mass., 1931) and E. M. Gagey in *Ballad Opera* (New York, 1937) have shown. Ramsay converted the 1725 version of his play into a ballad opera after the successful production of *The Beggar's Opera* in 1728. It is the later version of *The Gentle Shepherd* that has usually been reprinted, and scholars have mistakenly assumed that this was the original version. See, in particular, Martin, *op. cit.*, pp. 81–2.

[16] See Smith, *op. cit.*, pp. 129–34.

voiced his conviction that Italian opera was destroying all interest in English ballads and songs. There is more than a trace of patriotic bigotry in this essay, but Addison undoubtedly feared that Continental entertainments would drive English tragedy and comedy from the stage and that artistic standards would consequently decline. For Addison, the triumph of Italian opera over English tragedy, comedy and music would not have been only a blow to national pride, but quite literally the victory of nonsense over sense, as he himself states in *The Spectator* No. 13 (15 March 1711). He exposes some of the absurdities of Italian opera in *The Spectator* No. 5 (6 March 1711). Addison even tried to oppose Italian opera directly by producing a distinctly English opera in the Italian form, but *Rosamond* (1707) was not a success.

Gay himself wrote very little about Italian opera, but although he liked music and provided Handel with a libretto in 1718 or 1719 for a decidedly Italianate 'English Pastoral Opera', *Acis and Galatea,* he was not uncritical of Italian opera. He did not share Addison's doctrinaire neoclassical views, but he too loved English folk songs and was concerned about the partial displacement of a native tradition by the vogue for Italian music. He also saw the current infatuation with Italian opera as a threat to Augustan literary values, as is evident in a letter to Swift dated 3 February 1723:

> As for the reigning Amusement of the town, tis entirely Musick. real fiddles, Bass Viols and Hautboys not poetical Harps, Lyres, and reeds. Theres nobody allow'd to say I sing but an Eunuch or an Italian Woman. Every body is grown now as great a judge of Musick as they were in your time of Poetry. and folks that could not distinguish one tune from another now daily dispute about the different Styles of Hendel, Bononcini, and Attillio. People have now forgot Homer, and Virgil & Caesar, or at least they have lost their ranks, for in London and Westminster in all polite conversation's Senesino is daily voted to be the greatest man that ever liv'd.[17]

It was the uncritical response of the public to Italian opera that perturbed Gay. Lord Cobham's ironic suggestion that *The Beggar's Opera* should have been printed 'in Italian over against the English, that the Ladys might have understood what they read',[18] with its biting insight into fashionable theatre-goers, must have appealed greatly to him.

As the only member of the Scriblerus Club who wrote seriously and

[17] *Letters*, ed. Burgess, p. 43.
[18] *Ibid.*, p. 71. (Mentioned in a letter from Gay to Swift dated 15 February 1728.)

regularly for the stage, Gay was particularly disturbed about the state of contemporary theatre. In the Epilogue to his second and last tragedy, *The Captives* (1724), he implicitly defends the traditional dramatic forms by launching an ironical attack on two of the most modish theatrical entertainments of the day, operas and masquerades. In the circumstances it was almost inevitable that the finest writer of dramatic burlesque in the first thirty years of the eighteenth century should have joined battle with Italian opera. Bertrand H. Bronson, one of the best critics of *The Beggar's Opera*, believes that Gay did not intend 'a serious attack upon Italian opera' and that 'his ridicule does not go beyond poking affectionate fun' at operatic conventions,[19] but it is difficult to be certain of Gay's intentions. Whatever these were, *The Beggar's Opera* did not drive Italian opera from the London stage as has sometimes been thought, but it did deal conventional opera a blow by creating a new vogue for ballad operas and ballad farces.

Unlike earlier burlesquers of Italian opera such as Estcourt, Gay does not parody any particular opera or operas, nor does he attempt a comprehensive burlesque of all the features of opera. He does not burlesque operatic spectacle, for example, although Italian opera was very susceptible to an attack of this sort. He prefers to answer the extravagance of operatic productions with the restraint and austerity of his own 'opera'. Indeed his method of attacking Italian opera is almost always indirect and subtle, as might be expected from his earlier dramatic burlesques, but *The Beggar's Opera* is much more ambitious than *The Mohocks* and *The What D'Ye Call It*. In these works Gay is content to ridicule contemporary tragedy, whereas in *The Beggar's Opera* his burlesque of Italian opera is inseparable from his creation of a new kind of opera, specifically English in character and considerably closer to Restoration dramatic opera than to Italian opera in its deployment of music. *The Beggar's Opera* is therefore unique among dramatic burlesques in being planned as a rival of the form it criticises. Part of its purpose was to establish a form that would encourage ballad singers and stimulate an interest in English song. With the exception of the Overture, which was provided by the musical director of Rich's theatre, Dr Pepusch, in order to reinforce the burlesque resemblance to Italian opera,[20] none of the music was specially composed. Gay wrote the words for all sixty-nine Airs with well-known tunes in mind,

[19] '*The Beggar's Opera*', in *Studies in the Comic* (Berkeley and Los Angeles, 1941), p. 216. Also in *Restoration Drama: Modern Essays in Criticism*, ed. J. Loftis (New York, 1966), p. 314.

[20] For a fuller discussion of the Overture, see Commentary on the Introduction 29.

many of which were taken from Thomas D'Urfey's popular collection of 'the best merry Ballads and Songs, old and new', *Wit and Mirth: or Pills to Purge Melancholy* (6 volumes, 1719–20). Gay chose the tunes, mainly ballad tunes, with considerable care, and skilfully matched his own words to the music, occasionally retaining or adapting lines and phrases from his sources, as in Air XII ('*Oh, ponder well! be not severe*' based on 'Now ponder well, ye Parents dear') and Air XIV ('*Pretty* Polly, *say*' based on 'Pretty Parrot, say'). Many contemporary dramatists included a few incidental songs in their plays, but Gay broke new ground by giving the large number of Airs in *The Beggar's Opera* such prominence and importance. His songs are an integral part of the play and not incidental.

Gay could have devised an English antidote to Italian opera without recourse to burlesque. His own sequel to *The Beggar's Opera*, *Polly* (1729), like most of the ballad operas and ballad farces that appeared in such profusion during the 1730's and 1740's, can hardly be described as burlesque. But the ironical incongruity of the title, which links 'Beggar' with 'Opera', is sufficient to indicate that Gay was cocking a snook at Italian opera as well as resuscitating English opera, and at two points (Introduction and III. XVI) he explicitly ridicules Italian opera. By means of the Beggar's statement in the Introduction, 'I have not made my Opera throughout unnatural, like those in vogue', Gay implies that the world of his 'opera' is totally different from that of conventional opera, and he proceeds to burlesque Italian opera in exactly the same way as he had earlier attacked contemporary tragedy in *The Mohocks* and *The What D'Ye Call It*. While maintaining the pretence that he is offering a normal opera even to the extent of using the three-act structure usual in opera as opposed to the five-act structure standard in tragedy and comedy, he introduces a cross-section of low life completely out of keeping with the elevated tone usually associated with the form. In *The Beggar's Opera* time is measured by the sessions of the criminal court, and the outlook for most of the characters seems to be hanging or transportation. For the mythological or courtly setting of opera, Gay substitutes Newgate Prison and a group of thieves and prostitutes. For exalted heroes and heroines, he substitutes 'Captain' Macheath, the leader of a gang of highwaymen, and Polly Peachum and Lucy Lockit, the daughters of a receiver of stolen goods and a prison-keeper respectively. For noble actions, dignified emotions and refined language, he substitutes crime, double-dealing, lechery, callousness and the chatter of the underworld. Gay turns Italian opera on its head. Although this burlesque method is essentially the same

as that used by Thomas Duffett over fifty years earlier[21] and by Gay himself in his first two dramatic burlesques, Gay now seizes the opportunity of
adapting his mock-heroic reversals to social and political satire. In *The
Mohocks* Gay suggests how this could be achieved without making any
attempt to do so. In *The Beggar's Opera* his presentation of a highwayman as his 'operatic' hero is patently burlesque, but he uses this inversion
of values to expose the corrupt values of high society and of the Government.

Although the descriptions of Macheath as a 'Gentleman' and a 'great
Man' are in one sense deeply ironic, he is shown to be just as deserving of
such labels as many of those who are accepted in the beau monde, Parliament and the Army as fine gentlemen and great men. In generously
distributing his money to his gang, addressing them as 'Gentlemen',
talking about their 'Honour', and claiming that he has always been just
and equitable, the criminal Macheath is behaving like an aristocratic
operatic hero. The deliberate incongruity must be interpreted as ironic
burlesque. Yet at the same time this irony rebounds to satirise the pre-
tensions, hypocrisy, deceit and self-seeking of the upper classes and of
politicians. Throughout the play Gay exploits this two-way irony to
establish that the behaviour of outwardly respectable and reputable men
of position and power is often morally indistinguishable from that of
criminals. Indeed the behaviour of men in public life is really very much
worse because of the ingenious hypocrisy expended on disguising vice
as virtue, dishonesty as political necessity, and selfishness as patriotic
duty. By conventional standards Macheath is branded as a criminal, but
he proves by his generosity and service to his gang that he has more right
to talk about honour, justice and loyalty than most courtiers, politicians,
lawyers and military leaders of the real world. As the leader of a gang of
highwayman, he sees himself as the equivalent of an army officer and is
called 'Captain' throughout, but the implication is that he treats his
subordinates very much better than an officer would. Mrs Peachum feels
that it is wrong of Macheath 'to keep Company with Lords and Gentlemen' in the gaming-houses because they should be left 'to prey upon one
another', and Ben Budge, one of the gang, also expresses regret that
Macheath's fondness for gambling should lead him to associate 'with such
ill Company' as the upper classes. The numerous comparisons between
the underworld and 'the Quality' (including those between the whores in

[21] See V. C. Clinton-Baddeley, *The Burlesque Tradition in the English Theatre after
1660* (London, 1952), pp. 38–43. Also my 'The Three Dramatic Burlesques of
Thomas Duffett', in *Durham University Journal*, XXVII (1965–6), pp. 149–56.

the tavern scene and 'fine Ladies') are almost always to the detriment of the latter. 'Why are the Laws levell'd at us?' asks another member of the gang, Jemmy Twitcher, 'are we more dishonest than the rest of Mankind?' Macheath's gang has its own strict code of conduct that reveals the respectability of their 'betters' for the sham veneer it is. To use the distinction made by the Beggar, it is 'the Gentlemen of the Road' and not 'the fine Gentlemen' who, according to Macheath, 'have still Honour enough to break through the Corruptions of the World'.

Yet even though Macheath is in many ways an attractive and appealing character, an unconventional hero as well as an anti-hero, Gay avoids the danger of sentimentalising and romanticising the gang. His sustained irony ensures this. Despite the high-minded sentiments of the gang in II. I when they are justifying their way of life as an attempt to secure 'a just Partition of the World', they finally fail to live up to their own standards. Some of their exclamations and rhetorical questions about their mutual loyalty and their being 'above the Fear of Death' eventually ring hollow when Macheath is 'peached' by Jemmy Twitcher and behaves less than heroically in the condemned cell, relying on alcohol to keep his courage up. It is also significant that earlier in the play Macheath is betrayed by two of his women friends from the underworld, the prostitutes Jenny Diver and Suky Tawdry. Jemmy Twitcher's act of betrayal makes Macheath sad rather than angry because it means that the gang has sunk to the level of high society and of politicians, that 'the World is all alike'. The ironical implication, as in the best-known song in the play, '*The Modes of the Court so common are grown*' (Air XLIV), is that the corruption of the Court has spread to society as a whole and contaminated even honest, hard-working criminals. Another important factor is that in matters of love Macheath himself is a traitor, making false promises to both Polly and Lucy as a 'Man of Honour', although Gay is of course suggesting that those regarded by society as men of honour can behave just as badly, if not worse.

In handling the theme of love and marriage, Gay again makes his ironic burlesque reflect satirically on the moral vacuum at the heart of London's aristocracy and gentry. When Peachum and his wife discover that their daughter Polly has secretly married Macheath against their wishes, they question her about her reasons for marrying and suggest that the main one must be the hope of becoming a rich widow as soon as possible after the wedding. Following his wife's claim that Polly has married because 'she would do like the Gentry'—a little earlier Mrs Peachum asserts that Polly 'loves to imitate the fine Ladies'—Peachum puts it to his daughter that she holds 'the common Views of a Gentlewoman' about marriage, namely that it is a necessary step on the way to the 'comfortable Estate of Widow-hood'. To Polly's horror, her parents not only plan her husband's death but expect her, out of filial duty, to assist them. Peachum assures Polly that there is 'no Malice' in his proposals, simply good business sense. As far as the Peachums are concerned, love belongs entirely to the world of fiction and fantasy, to the romances and 'cursed Play-books', as Mrs Peachum calls them, that Polly reads and to some extent confuses with real life. In her naïvety, Polly identifies Macheath with 'great Heroes' and consequently and quite wrongly believes that he cannot be 'false in Love', but the quality and strength of her love are never in doubt, and are evinced by her defiance of her parents and by her independent and determined behaviour—Polly, who knows 'as well as any of the fine Ladies how to make the most of my self and of my Man too', is not the sentimental, milk-and-water heroine that some actresses have turned her into. By presenting a particularly jaundiced view of love and marriage as reasonable and normal in the speeches of Peachum and his wife (and in those of Lockit, whose daughter Lucy also loves Macheath and wants to marry him), Gay travesties the sacramental attitudes to love found in opera and the tender expectations of operatic heroines. But what in one way is burlesque is in another way stinging social satire. According to her mother, Polly 'wilt be as ill-us'd, and as much neglected, as if thou hadst married a Lord!', and when Polly explains that she has married for love, not '(as 'tis the Fashion) cooly and deliberately for Honour or Money', Mrs Peachum exclaims, before fainting from shock, that she 'thought the Girl had been better bred'. The travesty of the absurdly idealistic love in opera is simultaneously a picture of the unpleasant actualities of many high society marriages. Burlesque and social satire are inseparable.

Although Gay's burlesque is aimed primarily at Italian opera, some of it is equally applicable to contemporary drama, especially to the heroic and sentimental aspects of Restoration and Augustan tragedy, but also to the 'genteel' or 'sentimental' comedy of Cibber and Steele. The reason for this is that the burlesque is general rather than specific. In *The Mohocks* and *The What D'Ye Call It* Gay puts the speeches of hooligans and peasants into the idiom of contemporary tragedy in order to ridicule its stilted diction and inflated rhetoric, whereas in *The Beggar's Opera* he only occasionally makes his low-life characters converse in the heightened manner of opera. For these underworld figures to resort to song in the manner of operatic heroes and heroines does create considerable burlesque humour at the expense of Italian opera, but there is virtually no parody of particular recitatives and arias. Gay does not attempt any extended verbal burlesque of what Addison calls 'the forced Thoughts, cold Conceits, and unnatural Expressions'[22] of Italian opera because this would have been incomprehensible to an English audience. Except during the years immediately after their introduction into England, Italian operas were always sung in Italian, a language not widely known. The result is that Gay's burlesque also refers to the features of contemporary drama having something in common with Italian opera. There is even some verbal burlesque of 'sentimental drama', as in the scenes between Polly and Macheath at the end of Act I, although here as elsewhere their speeches are much more than burlesque.[23]

In conceiving some of his characters, Gay had in mind certain well-known contemporary criminals. He is usually said to have based Macheath on Jack Sheppard, the thief who became a legend during his short life because of the ingenuity and bravery with which he flouted the authorities. Before he was hanged in 1724, Sheppard managed to escape from Newgate on several occasions. When he was finally taken to execution at Tyburn, he was fêted as a popular hero by the lower classes, and his journey through the streets of London in the 'cart' became a triumphant procession. '*The Youth in his Cart hath the Air of a Lord*', a line in Air III, could almost be an allusion to Sheppard, although Gay's primary purpose is to establish the similarity between apparently dissimilar people, criminals and aristocrats. A romantic aura surrounds both Macheath and Sheppard, but the resemblance between them does not go much beyond this. Sheppard was a housebreaker rather than a highwayman, and he did not lead a gang.

Peachum is closely modelled on the much more sinister figure of Jonathan Wild, who was one of the most successful exponents of organised crime in the first half of the eighteenth century. Although he ran a gang of thieves and acted as a receiver for the goods they stole, Wild was also a thief-taker working hand-in-glove with the law. When it suited him, he betrayed members of his gang for the £40 reward paid to anyone supplying evidence that secured a conviction on a criminal charge. He even intimidated or bribed other members of the gang to testify against their colleagues. Yet in spite of this treacherous double-dealing, Wild was able to retain his gang and recruit new members. For one thing, he was indispensable to the gang because of his ability to dispose of what they

[22] *The Spectator* (No. 13), ed. D. F. Bond (Oxford, 1965), vol. I, p. 59.
[23] See Commentary on I. XII and on I. XIII.

stole. (In II. II Macheath reminds his gang that 'Business cannot go on without' Peachum and that they 'must continue to act under his Direction, for the moment we break loose from him, our Gang is ruin'd'.) Furthermore he could behave generously to criminals on good terms with him by attempting to secure their acquittal if they were apprehended and put on trial. He would establish alibis for them or arrange for vital evidence to be suppressed. Wild managed the gang's activities in a very business-like way, planning their operations carefully and keeping accurate accounts of stolen property, which he frequently returned to the rightful owners for the reward they offered. He even had arrangements for sending abroad stolen valuables that could not be disposed of in England without serious risk. For Wild, crime was indeed a business, and a very profitable one. The revelations made about him at the time of his trial and execution in 1725, which are recorded in Alexander Smith's *Memoirs of the Life and Times of the Famous Jonathan Wild* (1726) and other contemporary documents, caused widespread public interest and concern. Gay was indebted to the many popular accounts of the contemporary underworld and its most notorious figures such as those by Smith, but his comic and ironic handling of the subject-matter is totally different from the usual mixture of lurid sensationalism and moral platitudes.

Gay had previously written about Wild in a ballad called *Newgate's Garland* (originally *Blue-skin's Ballad*), which foreshadows *The Beggar's Opera* in a number of ways.[24] 'Blueskin' was the nickname of Joseph Blake, a robber and an associate of Wild who had nevertheless been 'taken' and brought to justice by Wild. During his trial in 1724 Blake attacked Wild and wounded him in the throat with a penknife. In *Newgate's Garland* Gay uses this famous courtroom incident as the basis for an ironic satire on financial malpractices and corrupt behaviour to be found throughout society, but especially in high places and among the professions:

> Some say there are Courtiers of highest Renown,
> Who steal the King's Gold, and leave him but a *Crown*;
> Some say there are Peers, and some Parliament Men,
> Who meet once a Year to rob Courtiers agen[.]   (19–22)

---

[24] Because this ballad was published anonymously, it is not certain that Gay wrote it, but it has usually been attributed to him. See G. C. Faber (ed.), *The Poetical Works of John Gay* (London, 1926), pp. xxvi–xxvii, and H. Williams (ed.), *The Poems of Jonathan Swift* (Oxford, 1937), vol. III, pp. 1111–3, for conflicting views about its authorship.

Knaves of old, to hide Guilt by their cunning Inventions,
Call'd Briberies Grants, and plain Robberies Pensions;
Physicians and Lawyers (who take their Degrees
To be Learned Rogues) call'd their Pilfering, Fees[.][25] (28–31)

As in *The Beggar's Opera* Gay morally equates courtiers, politicians, doctors and lawyers with thieves and highwaymen, 'Ye Gallants of *Newgate*'. Gay's interest in the underworld is also evident in one of his longest and most important poems, *Trivia; or, The Art of Walking the Streets of London* (1716), although his treatment is very different from that in the later works. The passages about pickpockets, prostitutes and ballad singers in *Trivia* are a mixture of objective description and conventional moralising.

Even though Gay implicitly identifies the Hanoverian Court, Whitehall and high society with a gang of highwaymen, Newgate and the underworld, no single character in *The Beggar's Opera* corresponds to Sir Robert Walpole (1676–1745), the leader of the parliamentary Whigs and chief Minister of State (effectively Prime Minister)[26] from 1721 until 1742. Nevertheless Gay embodies much of his condemnation of Walpole and his Whig administration in Peachum, who likens his own conduct to that of lawyers and politicians and frequently emphasises the close similarity between low life and high life, as in the song and soliloquy with which the play opens. Here as elsewhere Peachum claims that the standards of his 'Business' or 'Employment' are at least as 'honest' as those of the socially accepted professions. The way in which he and his wife try to behave like the gentry, keeping up appearances and showing concern for their family reputation and social position, heightens the social and political satire. Peachum appeals to 'the Rules of Decency', Mrs Peachum refers to her 'over-scrupulous Conscience', and her reaction to the news that her only child has married a highwayman is, 'Then all the Hopes of our Family are gone for ever and ever!' In all his dealings, including his arrest of Macheath in II. v, Peachum tries to maintain a polite but business-like attitude. Only in his quarrel with Lockit in II. x does this facade crumble completely, and it is quickly restored for the sake of their 'mutual Interest'.

[25] These and subsequent quotations from Gay's poems are taken from Faber's edition.
[26] The Cabinet Office of Prime Minister did not exist at this time. Strictly speaking, Walpole was Chancellor of the Exchequer and First Lord of the Treasury, but during his long period of power he increasingly took on the function of a Prime Minister.

If Macheath corresponds to the aristocracy, Peachum and Lockit corres-
pond to the bourgeoisie, the increasingly powerful Whig merchant class
of the eighteenth century. Peachum is the practical businessman, the hard-
headed and hard-hearted realist concerned for the most part with money
and governed by what is expedient. At only one point does he show any
sign of soft-heartedness, and even this momentary reluctance in I. XI to
arrange Macheath's death is partly motivated by financial considerations:
'When I consider . . . how much we have already got by him, and how
much more we may get, methinks I can't find in my Heart to have a Hand
in his Death'. Believing that love and marriage are matters of policy and
convenience, he callously regards Polly's love for Macheath as a kind of
madness or delusion. His cynicism is so deeply rooted that moral values
are meaningless to him, and he has no qualms about using bribery to
achieve his purposes. For Peachum, 'Murder is as fashionable a Crime as a
Man can be guilty of'. In his mouth, words change or lose their normal
meanings. He speaks of the executions he is planning as 'decent', calls
Slippery Sam a 'Villain' because he intends to abandon crime for 'an
honest Employment', and commends Nimming Ned for rescuing (i.e.
stealing) goods from fires. Such abuse of language pervades the play;
Peachum's 'apprentice' Filch, for example, talks of 'Penitence' as a fault
or weakness, Lockit calls bribery 'Civility', and Macheath says that
highway robbery has done him 'justice' meaning that it has been very
lucrative. The implication throughout is that the behaviour of Walpole
and other Whig leaders is no different from that of Peachum, except that
the corruption they practise is on a much larger scale. Walpole was often
accused of exploiting his position to acquire a fortune, and even at a time
when any successful politician realised the value of a well-placed bribe,
he was known to make particularly lavish use of corruption, treating it as
an instrument of government. Fielding followed Gay's example of using
Wild's career as the basis for satire on Walpole in his fictional *Life of
Mr Jonathan Wild the Great* (1743).[27]

Peachum is Gay's chief weapon in the armoury he uses against Walpole,
but satirical allusions to the Minister abound. Gay's ironic use of 'great'
and 'great Man' throughout the play, for example, is aimed at Walpole,
who was often referred to as 'The Great Man', especially by his political
opponents. Gay's exposure of the petty corruption rife in Newgate and of
the jailors' iniquitous abuse of power for personal gain is another way in
which he indirectly indicts Walpole and his administration; the chief

[27] For a comparison of the two works, see the essay by John Preston and the short
article by Robert A. Smith listed in the Bibliography.

jailor, Lockit, is very similar to Peachum and his partner in crime. There are also parallels between Robin of Bagshot and Walpole,[28] and even between Macheath and Walpole. Macheath, the leader of a gang of highwaymen, is involved with two women, just as Walpole, the leader of the Court party, was; he kept a mistress as well as a wife. Macheath and his gang are robbers of the public; it is implied that Walpole and his Government are too. Macheath's hairbreadth escape from death by a last-minute reprieve at the end of the play is primarily a burlesque of operatic dénouements, but it also alludes to Walpole's unexpected escape from political extinction after the death of George I and the accession of George II in 1727. Macheath, 'a great Man in Distress', survives, just as Walpole, another 'great Man in Distress', survived by promising the new King to increase the Civil List fund for the Royal Family's expenses.

Gay had a number of reasons for launching a full-scale attack on Walpole, the Government, the Court and high society. For one thing, he sided with the Tory Party, which had been in opposition since Queen Anne's death in 1714, and he shared the opinion of his great Tory friends, Pope, Swift and Arbuthnot, that Walpole was an unscrupulous rogue who was leading the nation into chaos and ruin. According to Sven M. Armens, Gay 'was a humanist upholding the Christian and classical values that he, Swift, and Pope sought to preserve in an age which they believed to be one of growing materialism, mechanism, and secularism, an age of weak morality and poor taste, an age of greed and injustice'.[29] Furthermore Gay's intimate experience of the Court and of high society convinced him that in general there was nothing to choose between the underworld and the aristocracy. If there was little honour among thieves, there was even less among those who constantly professed it. In a frank letter to Mrs Howard (subsequently Countess of Suffolk) written in August 1723, Gay makes some very disparaging remarks about statesmen, courtiers and 'great men', including an ironic comment that foreshadows *The Beggar's Opera*:

> I cannot indeed wonder that the Talents requisite for a great Statesman are so scarce in the world since so many of those who possess them are every month cut off in the prime of their Age at the Old-Baily.[30]

[28] See Commentary on I. III. 26–7 and on I. IV. 5.
[29] *John Gay, Social Critic* (New York, 1954), p. 217.
[30] *Letters*, ed. Burgess, p. 45.

Gay's final disillusionment with the 'great' world of the Court occurred when he was completing or had just completed the play. For some time he had been trying to obtain a more remunerative Court sinecure than the post of Commissioner of the State Lotteries he had held since 1723 with an annual salary of £150 and an apartment in Whitehall. Despite his low opinion of the Court, Gay enjoyed public office and aristocratic patronage, and to some extent was a place-seeker. This ambivalence towards the aristocracy and the Court frequently amused his literary friends. In 1727 he dedicated his *Fables* to Prince William (Duke of Cumberland) in the hope of a reward from his mother, Princess Caroline, who was shortly to become Queen after the death of George I in June 1727. As a result of his efforts Gay was offered a place at Court in October 1727, but this was the menial position of Gentleman-Usher to Princess Louisa, George II and Queen Caroline's youngest daughter who was only two years old. Gay was deeply wounded by what he regarded as a humiliating and insulting appointment at only £150 a year, and he turned it down. This disappointment came too late to affect the writing of *The Beggar's Opera*, but it must have convinced Gay that his satire of the Court was entirely justified.

In *John Gay, Social Critic* Sven M. Armens rightly argues that Gay's satire is not just an exposé of corruption in high life, as is often thought, but a panoramic survey of the distorted moral values and perverted human relationships produced at all social levels by urban life. For Gay, self-interest and greed are the main driving forces of urban society, from the aristocracy to the underworld, and money is both the principal goal aimed at and the standard for measuring success. The Peachums characteristically interpret Macheath's motive for marrying Polly as an attempt to obtain their wealth. References to money abound in the play—even Polly admits that she, like all women, 'knows how to be mercenary'—and 'Interest' is a key-word. Lockit, for example, tells Lucy, 'If you would not be look'd upon as a Fool, you should never do any thing but upon the Foot of Interest'. According to Peachum it is one of 'the Customs of the World' to 'make Gratitude give way to Interest', and Lockit claims that 'the Custom of the World' allows him to 'make use of the Privilege of Friendship' to cheat Peachum. Significantly, Lockit compares their behaviour to that of 'honest Tradesmen'. Ruthless competition is the norm, even between friends. This predominantly Hobbesian view of human society and relationships is most explicit in Lockit's soliloquy in III. II when he is planning to 'over-reach' Peachum: 'Of all Animals of Prey, Man is the only sociable one. Every one of us preys upon his Neighbour, and yet we herd together'. Gay shows that the pragmatic realism and reasonableness of worldly, self-centred men like Peachum and Lockit are identical to inhuman callousness and brutal indifference. Some of the animal images that pervade the play—men like '*Wolves*', Macheath like a '*Cock by Hens attended*', women like 'Decoy Ducks' deceiving men, gamblers like '*Pikes*' preying on one another, men like '*Gudgeons*' easily caught by women—help to define the ways in which human life is debased to the bestial. Such virtues as kindness, compassion, justice and charity are almost totally submerged beneath a pall of avarice, flattery, bribery and self-seeking, and it is not surprising that love is equated with sexual satisfaction and marriage regarded as an intolerable encumbrance. For many of the characters, sex is a commodity to be bought, sold or exploited. '*Suits of Love*', according to Filch, '*are won by Pay, | And Beauty must be fee'd into our Arms*', a view repeated by Macheath when he claims that every woman has her price since it is '*The Perquisite softens her into Consent*'. Most of the women in the cast are whores. Filch earns money from female prisoners in Newgate by making them pregnant so that they can 'plead their bellies' at their trials. Peachum exploits Polly's attractiveness in his business dealings. Mrs Peachum sees sex as the means by which a woman can obtain a wealthy husband. Polly is the only character virtually uncontaminated by her milieu, and despite her attempt to deceive her parents by concealing her marriage from them, she does approximate to an embodiment of sincerity and purity in an insincere and impure world. Yet although *The Beggar's Opera* is basically very serious, Gay's approach is never portentous or solemn, and he does not resort to self-righteous preaching. On the contrary, his satire is so successful because it is presented with such wit and vitality and because it is embodied in an extremely entertaining and superbly theatrical play. *The Beggar's Opera* is a profound satire and a lively musical comedy. It is also a moving but completely unsentimental love story. Like most great works of art, it can be appreciated and enjoyed at many levels.

In order to convey a world dominated by Hobbesian 'interest', Gay has constructed a plot that is a series of betrayals, deceptions and reversals. Polly deceives her parents by marrying Macheath without informing them. In spite of protesting that he 'would not willingly forfeit my own Honour by betraying any body', Filch breaks his promise to Polly not to reveal her marriage to her parents. Peachum and Mrs Peachum feel the marriage to be a threat to themselves, and although genuinely fond of Macheath and on excellent business terms with him—even when arresting Macheath, Peachum compares him to 'The greatest Heroes'—they decide to arrange his execution. At the end of Act I Macheath assures Polly of the strength and constancy of his love for her, but at the beginning of Act II he reveals that he loves 'the Sex', not just Polly, and that he 'must have Women', not one woman. He, a traitor in love, is in turn betrayed to Peachum by two of the eight whores he invites to join him at a tavern. He complains bitterly that women cannot be trusted, although he himself is false to Polly, and is surprised at Jenny Diver's involvement in his arrest, although he earlier describes her as 'a dear artful Hypocrite'. In Newgate, Macheath deceives Lucy, whom he has seduced and made pregnant, into believing that she is his true love. To do this he virtually has to disown Polly when she visits him in prison. He can then persuade Lucy to arrange his escape. Meanwhile Lockit is planning to outwit his colleague Peachum because he believes that Peachum is trying to swindle him out of his share of Macheath's wealth. Mrs Trapes accidentally betrays Macheath to Peachum and Lockit, but washes her hands of responsibility for the outcome when she realises that as a result she will be able to obtain what she wants from them. Under the guise of friendship and mutual commiseration, Lucy seeks to revenge herself on Polly by poisoning her. At Macheath's trial, Jemmy Twitcher gives evidence against his leader. Macheath exhibits fear rather than courage in the condemned cell until visited not only by Polly and Lucy but also by four other 'Wives' each with a child, when out of self-interest he suddenly finds that the prospect of being hanged is preferable to remaining where he is. Even the unexpected dénouement, in which the Beggar and the Player intervene to announce a reprieve for Macheath and to impose a happy ending, illustrates 'interest' in that it is introduced, as the Player explains, 'to comply with the Taste of the Town' and so secure commercial success for the Beggar's 'opera'.[31]

The artistic success of the play ultimately depends on Gay's thoroughgoing use of irony, established at the outset by his use of the 'mask' of the Beggar. This also enabled him to pillory the Court and the Government without coming into direct conflict with the authorities. The apparently light-hearted and politically innocent surface of *The Beggar's Opera* deceived no one, but Walpole and the Government could not take any action against the play without acknowledging that Gay's attack was implicitly directed against them. If Walpole had banned the play after it had reached the stage, he would have committed a grave political blunder by playing into the hands of the Opposition. Nevertheless *The Beggar's Opera* did offend the Court and the Whig administration very deeply,

[31] For a fuller discussion of the dénouement, see Commentary on III. XVI.

especially as it enjoyed such enormous success. When the Government learned that Gay had written a sequel to *The Beggar's Opera* and that a production of *Polly* was likely at the end of 1728 or early in 1729, Walpole decided to take the initiative by suppressing *Polly* before it could reach the stage. Walpole probably expected the sequel to be another whole-hearted attack on himself, the Court and the Government, but he was wrong. *Polly* is very different from *The Beggar's Opera* and might not have caused the Government any embarrassment if it had been produced. Even so, Walpole could not afford to take any chances after the success of *The Beggar's Opera*, and he obviously wanted to discourage Gay from writing more satirical plays. *Polly* was published in 1729 and sold extremely well, but the first production did not take place until 1777. *The Beggar's Opera* encouraged other dramatists, notably Fielding, to satirise Walpole in the theatre, and during the 1730's these attacks became more and more daring. Walpole finally brought them to an end by introducing strict control of the theatres and by imposing a severe censorship on the stage in the form of the Licensing Act of 1737. Gay himself continued to attack Walpole, the Government and the Court in the Second Series of his *Fables*, published posthumously in 1738.

Perhaps the most remarkable thing about *The Beggar's Opera* is that in spite of being so deeply rooted in the political and cultural situation of the 1720's it is a play of universal significance. In the last analysis it is irrelevant whether Gay was right or wrong about Walpole, who for all his faults and weaknesses was a gifted politician, a capable administrator and a skilful national leader. What is of lasting value is not the element of the party political tract, nor the numerous topical references, nor the burlesque of Italian opera, but the almost anarchic spirit in which Gay questions conventional assumptions, upsets normal expectations, and undermines orthodox social values and prejudices. By creating a topsy-turvy world in which a highwayman is a hero and criminals are shown to be less reprehensible than politicians and lawyers, Gay exposes the sandy foundations on which the status quo of public morality is established. He also subjects words like 'honesty', 'friendship', 'duty', 'honour' and 'gentleman' to a penetrating scrutiny that reveals the way in which they are often abused and rendered meaningless—his treatment of 'honest' at times recalls Shakespeare's handling of the word in connection with Iago in *Othello*. As a result Gay challenges his audiences and readers to examine and re-examine themselves and the world they live in. He does not allow us the luxury of wallowing in stock responses. Indeed throughout the eighteenth and nineteenth centuries moralists made vehement attacks on the play because they regarded it as an assault on accepted social, moral, religious and legal values, as a defence of the London underworld, and as a pernicious encouragement to vice and crime. These criticisms are based on a misconception of the play, as its notable defenders such as Swift in the eighteenth century and Hazlitt in the nineteenth century have pointed out,[32] but even though it would be misguided to think of Gay as a revolutionary, there is undoubtedly something socially and politically subversive about *The Beggar's Opera*. Gay's ostensibly comic vision of human life is fundamentally similar to his friend Swift's more explicitly tragic and pessimistic vision.

Largely because of the debate about its alleged immorality, more has probably been written about *The Beggar's Opera* than about any other English play except for those of Shakespeare. By far the most complete study is William Eben Schultz's *Gay's Beggar's Opera: Its Content, History and Influence* (1923), which examines every aspect of the play in considerable detail. Schultz also provides full documentation about the sources of the songs, a topic previously treated by A. E. H. Swaen (see Bibliography) and more recently discussed by Max Goberman in the facsimile reprint of the Third Edition.[33] Schultz's thorough and painstaking scholarship is invaluable, but his critical appraisal is disappointing. More satisfactory in this respect, although it needs to be treated with caution, is William Empson's long essay in *Some Versions of Pastoral* (1935), in which he employs his characteristic method of verbal analysis to elucidate Gay's subtle use of irony. Also important is Bertrand H. Bronson's refreshing essay first published in *Studies in the Comic* (1941) and now reprinted in *Restoration Drama: Modern Essays in Criticism* (1966). In *John Gay, Social Critic* (1954) Sven M. Armens makes an original approach to the play by relating it to some of Gay's poetry, such as *Trivia*, the *Epistles* and the *Fables*. Patricia Meyer Spacks's more recent book, *John Gay* (1965), also contains an interesting chapter on the play that is especially good on the animal imagery. Ian Donaldson's essay in his *The World Upside-Down: Comedy from Jonson to Fielding* (1970) contains some valuable suggestions, but parts of it read like an extension of Empson's essay, to which it is heavily indebted. The most important

---

[32] For a detailed account of these attacks on and defences of the play, see W. E. Schultz, *Gay's Beggar's Opera: Its Content, History and Influence* (New Haven, 1923), pp. 226–69.

[33] Claude M. Simpson's examination in *The British Broadside Ballad and Its Music* (New Brunswick, N.J., 1966) of the forty-one broadside ballad tunes used by Gay is even more authoritative, but he does not discuss the other twenty-eight tunes.

study of the burlesque element is probably Arthur V. Berger's essay, 'The Beggar's Opera, the Burlesque, and Italian Opera' (1936). Geoffrey Handley-Taylor and Frank Granville Barker's *John Gay and the Ballad Opera* (1956) is full of fascinating information, especially relevant pictorial material. An excellent edition of Gay's letters has recently (1966) been produced by C. F. Burgess, who has also written two helpful essays on the play, one on its genesis and the other on its political satire. The best biography of Gay is W. H. Irving's *John Gay, Favorite of the Wits*, first published in 1940.

II. THE TEXT

Considering that *The Beggar's Opera* is one of the pinnacles of English dramatic literature, it is surprising that no adequate bibliographical and textual analysis of the early editions has yet been published. The play has featured prominently in a bibliographical controversy about the significance of eighteenth century press figures,[34] and a few of its numerous editors, notably G. C. Faber, George H. Nettleton and Arthur E. Case, and Edgar V. Roberts (see Bibliography), have examined the text critically, but even these scholars leave much unsaid. The early editions present a particularly complex bibliographical problem, which Vinton A. Dearing alone has investigated with sufficient thoroughness,[35] but in spite of this there are comparatively few textual difficulties. Before Gay's death in 1732, three authorised editions were published in London, the First Edition (1728), the Second Edition (1728) and the Third Edition (1729). Each of these has a *prima facie* case to be considered authoritative, and their respective claims have to be carefully examined. At least four pirated editions were also published in Gay's lifetime, the so-called Third Edition (London, 1728) and three Dublin editions, the First (1728), Third

---

[34] See the articles by Philip Gaskell, Walter E. Knotts, and William B. Todd listed in the Bibliography. Knotts's pioneering attempt to identify the impressions of the First Edition is open to criticism on a number of counts, especially as it is based on a study of only eight copies, but Todd's hostile review is unnecessarily aggressive and harsh. Todd himself is open to criticism because his account of the impressions is not at all satisfactory.

[35] In preparing an authoritative edition of the play for his forthcoming Oxford edition of Gay's works, Dearing has collated copies of the early editions in major American libraries and in the British Museum. With three exceptions, my edition is based on copies in British libraries. Our investigations have been independent, but I am very grateful to Professor Dearing for providing me with the results of his bibliographical research, and I refer to them in this Introduction.

(1728) and Fourth (1732). There was possibly a Second Dublin Edition as well. These carry no authority but do shed light on a few editorial problems.

On 6 February 1728, just over a week after the first production on 29 January, Gay sold the copyright to the publishing-house of Tonson and Watts who rushed the play into print. The octavo First Edition (FE)[36] was on sale by 14 February, so it was probably produced in the short space of six working days. It was presumably set from a manuscript given to John Watts by Gay and therefore carries considerable authority. Basing his conclusions on a collation of twenty-six copies of FE, Dearing argues that there are five impressions (FE1–5), but some copies, especially three not examined by him, do not fit easily into this classification. Dearing himself notes that some copies of FE4, which presents a number of problems, are made up with odd sheets from other impressions. Nevertheless Dearing's classification is an essential basis for a bibliographical discussion of FE, and I adhere to it in this edition. Few copies of FE are identical, but an important reason for this is that several different sets of engraved plates were used for printing the music, some of which were modified during the press-run. If one ignores the music, five main states, corresponding to the five impressions, can be identified on the evidence of the press figures and other differences. As far as the actual play-text is concerned, exactly the same setting of type was used for FE1–4, and any differences are due to the failure of certain pieces of type to print in particular impressions, because of loss, damage, displacement, or lack of ink. The play-text in FE5 contains an extra song and a few corrections.

The title-page of FE1 reads: THE / *BEGGAR's* / OPERA. / As it is Acted at the / THEATRE-ROYAL / IN / *LINCOLNS-INN-FIELDS.* / [Rule] / Written by Mr. *GAY.* / [Rule] / — *Nos hæc novimus esse nihil.* Mart. / [Rule] / To which is Added, / *The* MUSICK *Engrav'd on* COPPER- / PLATES. / [Rule] / *LONDON:* / Printed for JOHN WATTS, at the Printing-Office / in *Wild-Court,* near *Lincoln's-Inn-Fields.* / [Rule] / MDCCXXVIII. / [Price 1s. 6d.]. The collation is: 8°:A^2, B–D^8, E^4, F^2, G–H^4. The following press figures are found in FE1: 1–B1^v; 2–C7^v, D7^v; 5–B4^v, D5^r; 8–E4^r. Skeleton formes were not used in this or later impressions of FE. The fifty-eight numbered pages of

---

[36] The sigla used in this Introduction and in the Textual Notes are mine, not Dearing's. I have used FE, SE, and TE, rather than the more conventional O1, O2, and Q, in order to make references to particular impressions and states of FE and SE as simple and unambiguous as possible.

text (B1^r–F1^v) are preceded by a title-page (A1^r), a page listing the Dramatis Personae and the actors in the first production (A1^v), and two pages devoted to the Introduction which is an integral part of the play (A2^{r-v}). An important feature is that the sixty-eight Airs printed in the text are numbered separately for each Act, I–XVIII for Act I, I–XXII for Act II, and I–XXVIII for Act III. In FE1 the catchword on E1^v is 'CENE' but should be 'SCENE'. The defective full-stop after 'Groves' on E3^v and 'a' in the last line of E1^v sometimes fail to print, and during the press-run a couple of unimportant punctuation marks not affecting the play-text were damaged or lost. The text of the play is followed by two pages of advertisements for books published by Tonson and Watts (F2^{r-v}) and by sixteen separately numbered pages of music giving the tunes for the Airs (G1^r–H4^v). Pepusch's Overture is not included. The music is printed from two pairs of engraved plates, one pair for signature G and the other pair for signature H. Each plate therefore contains four pages of music. I have examined six copies of FE1, including all those I have been able to find in British libraries: two in the Bodleian Library, Oxford (8°F259(8) Linc. and G.P. 930(3)—lacks F2 and signatures G–H); University Library, Cambridge (MR.463.c.70.2); Trinity College, Cambridge (W.10.69(pt. 2)); Beinecke Library, Yale University (IK. G252.728Bb); Wighton Music Collection, Dundee Public Libraries (72265 H—this problematic copy is discussed in the next paragraph). Dearing records six copies in American libraries: two in Harvard University; Yale University; Huntington Library; Library of Congress; University of Texas. One of the copies of FE in Edinburgh University Library (S* 28.7/3) is a mixture of FE1 and FE3, and is discussed under FE3.

In the copies of FE1 examined by Dearing and in five copies examined by me, the music is printed from the same pairs of plates, which may be called G^a and H^a. These are easily identified because the bottom stave of both G1^r and H1^r is blank. However in the copy in the Wighton Music Collection, signatures A–F are as in FE1 but signatures G–H are printed from different pairs of plates, G^b and H^b, which do not have a blank stave at the foot of G1^r and H1^r. According to Dearing, G^b and H^b were not used until FE4 and are the main distinguishing feature of that impression. Furthermore signature H in the Wighton copy is printed from H^b in an intermediate state of correction. Air 20 on H1^v has a key signature of three sharps on its first and second staves but a key signature of one sharp on its third stave. In one of the two copies of FE4 examined with signature H printed from H^b, the key signature is of one sharp throughout; in the other it is as in the Wighton copy. In the two copies of FE5 examined, the key signature is of three sharps throughout, which is correct. The Wighton copy is clearly an anomaly. Since G^b and H^b were not used for any other known copies of FE1–3, it is almost certain that they were not used in the printing of FE1. Signatures A–F of the Wighton copy were presumably laid aside until after the press-run of FE4 when signatures G–H were added to them to make a complete copy.

FE2 is a large-paper issue. Apart from the larger page size, FE2 is distinguished from FE1 by three features: the price is removed from the title-page; there is no press figure on $B1^v$—otherwise the press figures are the same; the catchword on $E1^v$ is corrected—'SCENE' instead of 'CENE'. The only copy of FE2 I have located in British libraries is in the British Museum (Ashley 3258). The only copy Dearing records in America is in the Huntington Library.

FE3 is a small-paper issue, the page size being the same as in FE1 and FE4–5. The price is restored to the title-page, but the setting differs slightly from that in FE1, the spacing of '$1s$' and '$6d$' being different. The press figures are totally different from those in FE2: 2–$B4^v$; 6–$C7^v$, $E4^r$, $F2^v$. Other differences from FE2 are caused by the loss or the failure to print of a few pieces of type, including 'as' at the beginning of the sixth line on $C8^r$, and the full-stops after '*Faints*' on $B6^r$ and 'Moral' on $F1^r$. The only copy of FE3 I have located in British libraries is in the British Museum (11775.c.45—lacks signatures G–H). The only copy Dearing records in America is in the Huntington Library. As has already been noted, a copy of FE in Edinburgh University Library (S* 28.7/3) is made up with sheets from FE1 and FE3. The evidence of the press figures establishes that signatures C–F are from FE1, but that signature B is from FE3. The setting of the price on the title-page establishes that signature A is also from FE3 (strictly speaking, it could be from FE4 or FE5, but considering the rest of the copy it is almost certainly from FE3). The music is printed from G^a and H^a.

With the exception of one anomalous copy (that in the Royal College of Music), FE4 is clearly distinguished from FE3 by the use of new plates for the music, although there are other differences. The only press figures are 2 on $C8^r$ (some copies) and 6 on $C8^v$ (all copies). Certain pieces of type that were lost from or failed to print in earlier impressions are replaced or restored, including 'as' on $C8^r$ and the full-stop after '*Faints*' on $B6^r$, and in most copies there is, for the first time, a hyphen between 'Snuff' and 'boxes' on $B2^r$ (see Textual Note on I. III. 7). Two pieces of type print intermittently—the defective full-stop after 'Groves' on $E3^v$

and the hyphen in 'a-peice' on $F1^r$. The changes in signatures G–H are much more considerable, as has been noted in the discussion of the Wighton copy of FE1. Except for the copy in the Royal College of Music, signature G is not printed from G^a but from G^b or G^c, two new pairs of plates, neither of which has a blank stave at the foot of $G1^r$. On $G3^r$ 'First' is engraved with a short 's' in G^b but with a long 's' in G^c; on $G4^v$ Air 13 occupies two staves in G^b but three staves in G^c. Signature H is printed from either H^a or H^b, a new pair of plates which does not have a blank stave at the foot of $H1^r$. In some copies H^a contains a correction, all four staves of Air 8 on $H2^v$ carrying a key signature of two flats; in other copies, as in earlier impressions, only the first two staves carry the key signature. I have examined seven copies of FE4, including all those I have been able to find in British libraries: Parry Room Library, Royal College of Music (II.G.4(1)—no press figure on $C8^r$; music printed from G^a and H^a, without the correction on $H2^v$); Edinburgh University Library (P. 187/3—no press figure on $C8^r$; music printed from G^b and H^a, without the correction on $H2^v$); Brotherton Collection, Brotherton Library, Leeds University (press figure on $C8^r$; music printed from G^b and H^a, with the correction on $H2^v$); Mitchell Library, Glasgow (782.6—lacks H4; no press figure on $C8^r$; music printed from G^b and H^a, with the correction on $H2^v$); two in the British Museum (Ashley 773—no press figure on $C8^r$; music printed from G^b and H^a, with the correction on $H2^v$: and C.71.d.10—lacks F2; signature C, lacking 'as' on $C8^r$ and with press figure 6 on $C7^v$ and none on $C8^{r-v}$, is from FE3; music printed from G^b and H^b, with the incorrect key signature for Air 20 on $H1^v$);[37] Houghton Library, Harvard University (Mus 500.2.3*(5)—press figure on $C8^r$; music printed from G^c and H^b, with the key signature of Air 20 on $H1^v$ partly corrected). Dearing records nine copies in American libraries: four in Harvard University; four in the University of Texas; Folger Shakespeare Library.

There are no press figures in FE5. The one major textual difference between FE5 and FE1–4 is the inclusion of the words and music of the song, *'Our selves, like the Great, to secure a Retreat'*, headed by 'A I R. A Cobler there was, &c.', on $E3^r$ (p.53) of FE5 (Air LVI in my edition). There can be no doubt that Gay wrote this song. Unlike the other songs this is not numbered, and the melody is printed from a wood-block, not from engraved copper-plates like the rest of the music. Up to and including $E2^v$, FE5 is virtually the same as FE4, although the play-text in FE5 contains four corrections which are discussed in the next paragraph.

[37] See the discussion of the Wighton copy of FE1 above.

The type for E3^r–F1^v in FE1–4 is used for FE5 but is reimposed to make room for the extra song. As a result the text in FE5 continues on to F2^r, replacing the advertisements on that page in FE1–4. In FE5 there is further replacement of lost or damaged punctuation, including the full-stop after 'Moral' on F1^v (on F1^r in FE1–4), but the full-stop after '*Eyes*' in Air XII on E2^r is missing. The music is printed from G^c and H^b.

T. J. Wise (see Bibliography) wrongly suggests that FE5 was the first impression and that the words and music of the unnumbered song were subsequently removed because the presence of three staves of music in the text was felt to spoil the appearance of the book. Wise fails to provide acceptable explanations of why the words were removed as well as the offending music, and of why the tune was not engraved with the others and printed at the end of the text, as one would expect if FE5 were the first impression. An examination of the four corrections in the play-text of FE5 proves conclusively that it was issued later than FE1–4. In FE1–4 Air XVI in Act I is incorrectly called 'VI', whereas in FE5 it is correctly numbered. Much more telling are the three corrections in Air XIV in Act III (Air LIV in my edition). In the eighth line of the song '*had*' in FE1–4 is replaced by the obviously correct '*bad*' in FE5, and twice in the song, in the third and fourth lines, 'Polly's' in FE1–4 is replaced in FE5 by 'Polly'*s*', which conforms to the typographical practice used throughout the text. These three corrections (unrecorded by previous editors) are particularly significant, not only because they could not possibly be corruptions, but also because they appear on E2^v which would have been side by side with E3^r in the forme. Since E3^r is the page on which the extra song is printed in FE5, E2^v would have been very easy to correct during the reimposition of E3^r. Other arguments are used by Walter E. Knotts (see Bibliography) to establish that FE5 is the final impression of FE. I have located two copies of FE5 in British libraries: British Museum (Ashley 3257); National Library of Scotland (Glen. 172(1)). In both of these the key signature of Air 20 on H1^v (three sharps throughout) and the time signatures of Air 20 on H4^r (6/8 instead of 3/4) and of Air 27 on H4^v (3/2 instead of 3/4) are corrected, but H^b is not fully corrected in all copies of FE5 (see Knotts, *op. cit.*, p. 211). Dearing records four copies in American libraries: two in Harvard University; Huntington Library; Clark Memorial Library. He notes that in one of the Harvard copies (15459.628.18*) there is a factotum at the beginning of the first line of Air I in Act I on B1^r instead of the ornamental initial found in all other copies of FE.

The octavo Second Edition (SE) was on sale by 9 April 1728, less than two months after the publication of FE1. Dearing has identified six issues of SE, but there are at least nine clearly defined states, almost certainly corresponding to nine issues (SE1–9). The title-page of SE1 is identical to that of FE3–5 except for the section between the epigraph and the imprint. This reads: [Rule] / The SECOND EDITION, / WITH THE / MUSICK *prefix'd to each* SONG. / [Two rules]. The collation of SE1 is: 8°: A⁴, C⁴, D–G⁸, H². There are no press figures in SE1, and skeleton formes were not used in this or later issues of SE. The seventy-six numbered pages of text (C1ʳ–H2ᵛ) are preceded by a title-page (A1ʳ), a page carrying a book advertisement headed '*March* 27, 1728' (A1ᵛ), three pages devoted to 'A / TABLE of the SONGS' (A2ʳ–3ʳ), a page listing the Dramatis Personae and the actors in the first production (A3ᵛ), and two pages for the Introduction (A4ʳ–ᵛ). The idea of providing the Table of Songs, which lists the first lines and not the titles of the tunes, must have occurred to either Gay or the publishers because of their great popularity. In SE, unlike FE, the tune of each song is printed immediately before the words, and the Airs are numbered consecutively throughout the text from I to LXIX. In addition two rules replace a single rule between scenes; the headlines include the Act number as well as the page number; and the running titles are set substantially in upper-case type ('The *BEGGAR*'s OPERA' as opposed to '*The* Beggar'*s Opera*' in FE). In spite of these differences, most of the type set for FE was not distributed but used again for SE. The type for signature A in FE5 (title-page, Dramatis Personae, and Introduction) was used unchanged for SE1 except for the modification of the title-page. The type for the body of the text had to be reimposed to allow for the different lay-out of the music, but that for B1ʳ–E1ʳ (pp. 1–49) in FE5 was used again for C1ʳ–G3ᵛ (pp. 1–62) and the top of G4ʳ (to the middle of Air L) in SE1. Some errors and omissions in these pages of FE5 were corrected in SE1 and a few minor modifications made for various reasons. The type for E1ᵛ–F2ʳ (pp. 50–59) in FE5 was not used for SE1.

During the reimposition of B1ʳ–E1ʳ of FE for SE1, a few substantive changes were made. The word order of the last sentence in I. VI was changed; '*have*' was introduced into the first line of Air VII; and an entire sentence was added immediately after Air XXIV in II. IV. The presence of these changes, which are undoubtedly authorial, indicates that before the imposition of SE1 the text of FE was checked, presumably against an authoritative manuscript, so that any deficiencies and defects could be rectified. In addition to the substantive changes, over twenty minor alterations were made. Some of these are corrections of obvious errors in

FE (the three changes in punctuation in I. IX and III. VIII, and 'su-/spect' for 'sus-/spect' in II. XV), but most were made in the interest of consistency. These include the capitalisation of the initial letters of twelve words, the italicisation of 'London', 'Irish', and 'South-Sea' in the song headings of Airs XXXIII, XXXIX, and XLII (presumably owing to an oversight, 'Irish' is not italicised in the song heading of Air XXXVI), and the spelling change of 'gray' for 'grey' in the song heading of Air II ('Gray' is the spelling in the song heading of Air I in both FE and SE). It is impossible to know for certain whether all of these changes have manuscript authority, but they are more likely to be authorial than the whim of the printers.

The existence of substantive changes suggests that the printers were provided with a list of corrections to make, and since they did not have to re-set the type, except for the numbers of the Airs, they would almost certainly have followed their instructions and left it at that. If they had made alterations on their own initiative, it is far more likely that they would have changed the setting of the Dramatis Personae at the beginning of I. VIII and of II. III from italic to roman type, which is used at the beginning of every other scene, than that they would have introduced capital letters in twelve words scattered throughout the text, indented every other line in Air VI, and hyphenated 'Knight Errant' in III. III. The two changes most likely to have been made by the printers on their own initiative were the removal of the full-stop after 'A I R' from the song headings of Airs XII and XXII of Act II in FE (Airs XXX and XL in SE) during the re-setting of the numbers. The normal typographical practice in FE is 'A I R' followed by the number, but in three cases 'A I R.' is found. Only one of these survives in SE, that in the song heading of Air XXVII (Air IX of Act II in FE). As a result of all these changes, this part of SE1 is textually superior to the corresponding part of FE, even though a few inconsistencies in capitalisation and italicisation survive in SE1, as do a couple of errors—'Chorus,' instead of 'Chorus.' at the end of the final stage-direction in II. II, and 'Mackheath' instead of 'Macheath' at the beginning of II. VII. In addition three punctuation marks were lost during the reimposition: the comma after '*born*' in Air XLVII, and the question mark after '*do*' and the full-stop after '*pursue*' in Air XLIX.

Also of interest are the six modifications in lineation made during the reimposition, only one of which was necessitated by the introduction of new type. In three cases a short word or syllable ('off' in II. IV, '-nour' in III. VI, and 'you' in III. VII) having a line to itself in FE was incorporated in the preceding line in SE1 to make room for the last line of an Air or stanza of an Air at the foot of the page. Another case is similar. A short line of dialogue and a short stage-direction in II. VI occupying a line each in FE were printed on the same line in SE1 to accommodate the final line of a speech at the foot of the page; '*Exeunt*' had to be shortened to '*Exe.*' to make this possible. In the remaining case, the title of the tune for Air VI was relineated slightly, presumably to improve its ungainly setting in FE. The modifications to Air I on the first page of Act I—the use of an unornamented large initial at the beginning of the first line and the change from a display to an orthodox lay-out—were presumably made because of the introduction of music on that page in SE1. The slight modification to Air XXVII (Air IX in Act II in FE), involving less indentation of two lines, must also have been made for aesthetic reasons.

The last part of SE1 is much less satisfactory than the rest of the text. In re-setting the type for G4ʳ (from the middle of Air L)–H2ᵛ (pp. 63–76), the compositors used FE5 as their copy. They corrected the numbering of Scene IX in Act III, wrongly called 'X' in FE, but the existence of some glaring errors not present in FE5 indicates that they did the work carelessly. 'Sprits' at the top of G4ᵛ and '*Canons*' in Air LV on G6ᵛ are misspellings of 'Spirits' and '*Cannons*'. Lockit's speech before Air LVI on G6ᵛ ends with a comma ('Whining,'). A full-stop ('*string.*') is erroneously inserted at the end of an enjambed line in Air LXVII on G8ᵛ. A stage-direction ('*Aside*') is omitted from the closing speech of III. X on G4ᵛ. Also omitted are the full-stops after 'compassionate' on G5ᵛ and after 'about' near the foot of H1ᵛ; the question mark after '*me*' in Air LIII on G5ᵛ; and the hyphen between '*Old*' and '*Baily*' near the top of G7ʳ— '*Old-Baily*' is hyphenated elsewhere in the text. The two changes in Air LVII on G7ʳ—'*the Lawyers*' and '*Lives,*' for '*The Lawyers*' and '*Lives.*' in FE—are almost certainly compositorial, not authorial. The compositors of the pirated Third Dublin Edition, which follows FE5, made exactly the same changes in this song; the compositors of the First Dublin Edition, which follows FE1–4, made the first of these two changes. The readings of SE seem more natural to a twentieth century eye, but the compositor who set this part of FE took more care than the compositor who re-set it for SE, and the readings of FE are therefore much more likely to be those of Gay's manuscript. The recurrence of almost all of these errors in SE2–9 means that the text of SE1 was not carefully examined and corrected before the printing of the later issues, even though a few corrections were made. The only other change in these pages, that of 'Heart' in Lucy's first speech on G5ʳ for 'heart' in FE, may have had manuscript authority. The usual form is 'Heart', as in Lockit's first speech at the top of the same page, and the existence of twelve similar changes in

C1^r–G3^v suggests that this was an authorial emendation. I have located two copies of SE1 in British libraries: Dyce and Forster Auxiliary Collection, Victoria and Albert Museum (F.D.10.32); Sheffield University Library (*822.56). Dearing records two copies in America, both in Harvard University Library.

Most of what has been said about SE1 is also true of SE2–9. The title-page of SE2 is identical to that of SE1 except for the section between the epigraph and the imprint. This reads: [Rule] / The SECOND EDITION: / To which is Added / The OUVERTURE in SCORE; / *And the* MUSICK *prefix'd to each* SONG. / [Two rules]. The collation of SE2 is: 8º: A–C⁴, D–G⁸, H². Pepusch's Overture, not included in SE1, occupies the whole of signature B, the eight pages being numbered independently of the rest of the book.[38] Otherwise SE2 is virtually the same as SE1, although '*wary*' replaces '*weary*' in Air XL on F4^v (see Textual Note on II. xv. 33), and the semicolon after '*shown*' in Air XXXVII on F3^r is missing. I have located two copies of SE2 in British libraries: National Library of Ireland (82256 g1); Cambridge Drama Collection, Nottingham University Library (s/PR 1269.G2). Dearing records two copies in American libraries: Harvard University; Yale University.

What distinguishes SE3 from SE2 is the presence of an extra advertisement headed '*May* 24, 1728' on A1^v. SE2 must have been on sale before this date and SE3 shortly after it. Otherwise SE3 is identical to SE2 except for the absence of 's' from 'see' at the beginning of the third line on G7^v, and the emendation of four errors in SE1–2: 'Sprits' is changed to 'Spirits' on G4^v; and the three punctuation marks lost during the reimposition of the type for SE1 are replaced, although a colon is used after '*pursue*' in Air XLIX on G3^v, not a full-stop as in FE. The only copy of SE3 I have located in British libraries is in the Brotherton Collection, Brotherton Library, Leeds University. Dearing records two copies in America, both in Harvard University Library.

The following press figures are found in SE4: 8–D5^v, E6^v, F3^r. The type of SE3 was rather carelessly reimposed for SE4 so that several dislocations occurred. C4^v (p. 8) lacks its page number, D8^r (p. 23) is numbered '230', and G2^r (p. 59) is numbered '95'. 'Exeuction' replaces 'Execution' at the bottom of C2^r; punctuation marks are lost from the ends of lines on E8^v (comma after 'can'), F3^v (comma after 'now'), and G5^v (full-stop after '*ill*' in Air LIII); 'T' is missing from the end of the

---

[38] The absence of signature B from SE1 means that the printers planned SE with the intention of including the Overture, but that for some reason this was not available when SE1 went to press.

sixth line on G4ᵛ; and the catchword is lost from F1ʳ. Nevertheless three emendations are found in SE4: a punctuation mark missing from SE2–3, the semicolon after '*shown*' in Air XXXVII on F3ʳ, is replaced by a colon; the 's' absent from 'see' on G7ᵛ in SE3 is restored; and the full-stop after '*string*' in Air LXVII on G8ᵛ in SE1–3 is removed. The only copy of SE4 I have located in British libraries is in the British Museum (11775.c.46). Dearing records two copies in America: Folger Shakespeare Library; Clark Memorial Library.

SE5 is clearly distinguished from SE4 by the insertion of an extra leaf without signature between signatures A and B. This leaf, headed 'The Names of the *Lilliputians*', contains a list of the actors and the parts they played in the sixteen performances given during the 1728–9 season by a company of child-actors called the Lilliputians; the verso is blank. Since the first performance by this company took place on 1 January 1729, SE5 could not have been issued until that month. The inclusion of this sheet in SE5 is indicative of the great interest aroused by the Lilliputian production. Other differences from SE4 are: (i) there is no press figure on D5ᵛ—otherwise the press figures are the same; (ii) the page numbering is corrected; (iii) G4ʳ is re-set, but without any significant changes; (iv) 'I' is restored to G4ᵛ; (v) new corruptions include '*reeurns*' for '*returns*' in the stage-direction at the foot of D6ʳ; the loss of punctuation marks from the ends of lines on D6ʳ (comma after 'abroad') and E2ᵛ (full-stop after 'Drawer' and comma after 'Ladies'); and the absence of 'he' from the end of the sixth line on E3ᵛ. The only copy of SE5 I have located in British libraries is in the Henry Watson Music Library, Manchester Public Libraries (BR 201 Pj22). Dearing makes no mention of SE5.

In SE6 'The Names of the *Lilliputians*' are not printed on a super-numerary leaf, as in SE5, but on A4ʳ, side by side with the original list of Dramatis Personae and actors; there are two corrections, '*Woodward*' for '*Wodward*' and a full-stop after 'Dolly Trull'. This necessitated the re-setting of the Introduction to make it fit on one page (A4ᵛ) in SE6; two minor changes were made by the compositors, 'my self, for 'myself' and 'Scene,' for 'Scene'. Five other changes in SE6 are probably non-authorial emendations of Gay's occasionally unorthodox spelling and punctuation: '*Lillies*' for '*Lillys*' in Air III on C3ʳ; 'Fellow.' for 'Fellow,' near the foot of E3ʳ; '*divide*' for '*divide,*' in Air XXXIX on F4ʳ; 'satisfy' for 'satisfye' near the top of G2ʳ; and 'me. 'Tis' for 'me, 'Tis' also on G2ʳ. Other differences from SE5 are: (i) there are no press figures; (ii) several cor-ruptions are corrected: 'Execution' replaces 'Exeuction' (found in SE4–5) on C2ʳ; '*returns*' replaces '*reeurns*' on D6ʳ; 'he' is restored to E3ᵛ; and the punctuation marks missing from F3ᵛ and G5ᵛ in SE4–5 are replaced; (iii) the catchword missing from F1ʳ in SE4–5 is replaced, but by the wrong word ('AIR' instead of 'SCENE'); (iv) other new corruptions include the insertion of 'It' at the end of the last line on E7ʳ; the numbering of F3ʳ (p. 45) as '54'; the replacement of 'Act III' by 'Act II' in the headline on G5ᵛ; and the absence of punctuation marks from the ends of lines on F2ᵛ (comma after *'refuse'* in Air XXXVI) and G7ᵛ (full-stop after 'Drinks'). I have located two copies of SE6 in British libraries: Bodleian Library (Vet.A4 e.311); Worcester College, Oxford (AA.5.3). Dearing records four copies in American libraries: Yale University; Huntington Library; Newberry Library; University of Chicago.

In SE7, F2ᵛ and F7ʳ are re-set and the lay-out of G4ʳ is slightly modified, but the compositors made only minor changes. On F2ᵛ there is a comma after *'refuse'*, as in SE1–5; the third speech-prefix from the bottom is *'Poll'*, not *'Polly'* as in SE1–6; and in the final speech 'your self' replaces 'yourself', found in SE1–6. Near the top of F7ʳ 'called' replaces 'call'd', found in SE1–6. Several corruptions introduced in SE6 are eliminated: 'It' is removed from E7ʳ; the page number of F3ʳ is corrected; the full-stop is restored to G7ᵛ (after 'Drinks'); and the incorrect catchword on F1ʳ is removed but not replaced. New corruptions include *'apears'* for *'appears'* in Air XXI on E2ʳ, and the replacement of 'Act II' by 'Act III' in the headline on E6ᵛ. The only copy of SE7 I have located in British libraries is in Worcester College, Oxford (LL.3.10). Dearing makes no mention of SE7.

In SE8 the decorative headbands of Acts I and III on C1ʳ and F5ʳ are changed, that on F5ʳ (emblems of music and two angels instead of emblems of war) being completely new, but that on C1ʳ (two dogs and an urn instead of a basket) being the same as that of Act II on D8ᵛ in SE1–8. Other differences from SE7 include 'a-piece' for 'a-peice' on H1ᵛ (see Textual Note on III. xv. 22); the restoration of the comma missing from E8ᵛ in SE4–7; the replacement of 'Act II' in the headline on G5ᵛ in SE6–7 by the correct 'Act III'; and the absence of the comma from the end of the first line on E4ᵛ and of the first 'i' from 'imitate' at the top of H2ʳ. I have located four copies of SE8 in British libraries: University Library, Cambridge (Syn.7.72.26¹—lacks A1 and A4); Lincoln College, Oxford (O.11.1(J)); London Library (L. ENGLISH DRAMA); Bath Municipal Libraries (822.56). Dearing makes no mention of SE8.

In SE9 there are a number of changes in the preliminaries. The price is omitted from the second advertisement on A1ᵛ, and the Table of Songs (A2ʳ–3ʳ) is substantially re-set. The running headlines on A2ᵛ and A3ʳ read 'A TABLE of the SONGS', not 'A TABLE of the AIRS' as in SE1–8, and there are several minor alterations such as *'Ore'* and *'Flow'r'* instead of *'Oar'* and *'Flower'* on A2^r and *'Traitors'* and *'ere'* instead of *'Traytors'* and *'e'er'* on A2^v. A3^v is also re-set, a full-stop replacing the comma found in FE and SE1–8 after 'Harry Padington', and the incorrect 'Snky Tawdry' replacing 'Suky Tawdry'. The decorative headband of Act I on C1^r (two dogs and an urn) is as in SE8, but that of Act II on D8^v (an angel) is completely new, and that of Act III on F5^r is as in SE1–7 (emblems of war). There are four probably non-authorial emendations: *'Lilies'* for *'Lillies'* in Air XXI on E2^r; 'Vultures' for 'Vulturs' on F6^v; 'Trial' for 'Tryal' also on F6^v; and 'Livelihood' for 'Livelyhood' on F7^r. Other differences from SE8 include the replacement of 'Act III' on E6^v in SE7–8 by the correct 'Act II'; the restoration of the correct catchword 'SCENE' to F1^r and of the first 'i' to 'imitate' on H2^r; and the loss of punctuation marks from the ends of lines on C2^r (comma after 'Gang'), D4^r (full-stop after 'consider'd'), and E3^r (full-stop after 'Fellow'). I have examined two copies of SE9, including the only one I have been able to find in British libraries: Rowe Music Library, King's College, Cambridge (Rw.86.15A); Houghton Library, Harvard University (15459.628.65*). The latter is the only copy recorded by Dearing.

What led the publishers to issue SE so soon after FE was the unflagging success and popularity of the play during its first season. What led them to issue the quarto Third Edition (TE) in 1729 was their publication of *Polly* in that year. The banning of *Polly* from the stage aroused widespread curiosity in this sequel to *The Beggar's Opera*, and the publishers made the most of this opportunity by issuing the play in a large, handsome and expensive volume. TE was produced as a companion volume to the first edition of *Polly* with the same format, design and typography. Its production, involving the use of skeleton formes, is therefore completely different from that of FE and SE. The collation is: 4°:A–H⁴, I², 2A–2E⁴, 2F², 2G1. The sixty numbered pages of text (B1^r–I2^v) are preceded by a title-page (A1^r), a blank page (A1^v), 'A / TABLE of the SONGS' as in SE (A2^r–A3^r), the Dramatis Personae and the actors in the first production (A3^v), and the Introduction (A4^{r-v}). The music, including the Overture, is printed *en bloc* after the text on forty-six separately numbered pages (2A1^r–2G1^v). Because of its splendid appearance, TE looks more authoritative than the comparatively cramped FE and SE, and most editors have regarded it unquestioningly as the most authoritative of the early editions. Yet appearances can be deceptive in bibliography as elsewhere, and even though TE is musically superior to FE and

SE, the text is another matter. Instead of giving only the basic tunes for the songs like FE and SE, TE provides a musical score showing how each syllable is related to each note of music and how the tunes are slightly modified at times to fit the words. The bass lines composed by Pepusch to provide harmonic foundations for the accompaniments are also given. This invaluable score, which shows exactly how the Airs were sung in early performances and is therefore very helpful to modern producers, is now readily available, thanks to the recent photographic reprint of TE ('46' in the Bibliography).

The text of TE, unlike the music, carries less authority than FE and SE. The perpetuation in TE of corruptions introduced in the re-set final part of SE1 that remain uncorrected in SE2–9, most significantly the omission of a stage-direction, '*Aside*', from III. x, of a question mark after '*me*' in Air LIII in III. xi, and of a hyphen between '*Old*' and '*Baily*' also in III. xi, establishes that TE was set from SE, not from an authoritative manuscript nor from a copy of SE that had been corrected from a manuscript. The compositors of TE almost certainly used one of the earlier issues of SE as their copy, probably SE4, which is closer to TE in a few points of detail than are SE1–3. Like SE1–4, TE lacks the list of Lilliputian actors incorporated in SE5–9, and although there are instances in which TE resembles some of the later issues of SE more closely than SE4 in punctuation and spelling, there are even more instances in which it does not. For example, TE contains two punctuation marks found in II. III in SE1–4 but not in SE5–9, and three of the five emendations introduced in SE6 and present in SE7–9 as well are not found in TE. In setting TE, the compositors made numerous minor departures from their copy-text. They used capital letters at the beginning of words much less frequently than in FE and SE, and this results in TE having a more modern appearance than the earlier editions. In addition the punctuation and spelling in TE are occasionally more orthodox and regular than in FE and SE and therefore appear more correct today (e.g. 'Gang.' for 'Gang,' (except in SE9 in which the comma is missing) in I. III; '*Lillies*' (also in SE6–9) for '*Lillys*' and '*Marybone*' for '*Mary-bone*' in I. IV— '*Marybone*' is the form found in I. VI, III. IV (twice), and III. VI in all three editions; '*ears.*' for '*Ears,*' in II. III; '*duty;*' for '*Duty,*' in II. IV; 'set' for 'sett' in II. VII; '*cries*' for '*crys*' in II. X; '*divide*' (also in SE6–9) for '*divide,*' in II. XIV; '*Sot:*' for '*Sot.*' in III. I; 'say I' for 'say, I' in III. VII; 'glimmer-ing' for 'glimm'ring' in III. X—'glimmering' is the form found in I. XIII in all three editions; and '*met;*' for '*met,*' in III. XI), but there is nothing to suggest that Gay either authorised or approved of these and the other minor alterations. In spite of the changes just mentioned, careful textual analysis of TE does not support Faber's claim that TE 'is more carefully considered' than FE and SE.[39] On the contrary, TE is more corrupt than the earlier editions.

With few exceptions the use of capital letters in SE is consistent, whereas it is erratic in TE with capitals sometimes not being used where they should be. 'Black *Moll*' (I. II and III. II) and 'Beetle-brow'd *Jemmy*' (I. VIII) are nicknames and should not be 'black *Moll*' and 'beetle-brow'd *Jemmy*' as in TE. Both 'Court' and 'court' appear in TE, and 'Captain' Macheath is sometimes 'captain' and sometimes 'Captain', which is preferable. Such glaring inconsistencies and incongruities are not present in FE and SE, with the exception of 'curl-pated *Hugh*' in II. X (also in TE and presumably in Gay's manuscript) instead of 'Curl-pated *Hugh*'. Many of the changes in spelling are also haphazard and inconsistent. In I. XIII 'rivited' in FE and SE is altered to 'riveted' in TE, but in II. IV 'rivetted' in FE and SE is altered to 'rivitted' in TE. All three editions give 'Ginn' in III. VI and III. VII, but in II. IV 'Ginn' in FE and SE is altered to 'gin' in TE. In II. XIII 'could' and 'show' in FE and SE are replaced in TE by 'cou'd' and 'shew', changes away from consistency, as are 'perswade' for 'persuade' in I. IV and 'Wou'd' for 'Would' in III. VIII, even though 'shew' is found in III. VIII, 'perswade' in III. VI, and 'Wou'd' in II. VIII ('wou'd' in TE) in all three editions. In II. IX '*Through*' in FE and SE is abbreviated to '*Thro*'' in TE, although the unabbreviated form is retained elsewhere. Similarly the last word in I. I in FE and SE, 'them', is altered to ''em' in TE, the only such abbreviation introduced in TE, which otherwise follows FE and SE exactly as regards 'them' and ''em'. In I. VIII 'reduc'd' in FE and SE is expanded into 'reduced' in TE, a departure from the normal practice employed. All three editions give 'satisfy' in I. II, but 'satisfye' in III. VI in FE and SE1–5 (SE6–9 give 'satisfy') is altered to 'satisfie' in TE, an odd change compared with that in SE6–9. And the spelling of 'livelihood', though slightly more consistent in TE than in FE and SE, is still inconsistent: in I. IV FE gives 'livelihood', SE 'Livelihood', and TE 'livelihood'; in I. IX FE and SE give 'Livelihood' and TE 'livelihood'; in II. X FE and SE give 'Livelyhood' and TE 'livelyhood'; and in III. III 'Livelyhood' in FE and SE (except for SE9 which gives 'Livelihood') is altered to 'livelihood' in TE. Indeed many possible modifications that one might expect to have been made if Faber's contention is correct, including some of the emendations introduced in SE6, SE8 and SE9, were not made in TE. All three editions give 'whimpring' in I. IV, but 'whimpering' in II. XI; 'handsomely' in II. IV and III. I, but 'handsomly' on two occasions in II. VII; and 'poysoning' in III. VII, but 'poison'd' in III. X. All three give '*listning*' in I. XI, 'Barr' in II. III ('barr' in TE), 'Vulturs' in III. II (SE9 gives 'Vultures'), '*agen*' in III. V, and '*threatning*' in III. XIII. Emendations that could have been made and that were made in subsequent eighteenth century editions, such as '*Ore*' for '*Oar*' in I. V '(*oar*' in TE), 'Ere' for 'E'er' in II. IV, 'borne' for 'born' in II. X, '*ere*' for '*e'er*' in II. XI, 'through' for 'thorough' in III. III, 'mere' for 'meer' in III. IV, and 'a-piece' for 'a-peice' in III. XV (this emendation does appear in SE8–9) were not made in TE. In addition many of the changes in punctuation and hyphenation are completely arbitrary, such as 'service:' for 'Service;' in I. III, 'sea-men' for 'Seamen' in I. VI, 'highway-man' for 'Highwayman' in I. VIII, and '*pill:*' for '*Pill;*' in II. VIII. A few words that are hyphenated in FE and SE ('ill-us'd' and 'Repeating-Watch' in I. VIII, and 'Winter-wear' in III. VI) are not hyphenated in TE, whereas some that are not hyphenated in FE and SE ('Hen Partridges' in I. II, 'Marriage Articles' in I. X, '*Surgeon*'s *Hall*' in II. I, and 'Hackney Coach' in III. VI) are hyphenated in TE. In some cases the punctuation in TE is distinctly less satisfactory than in FE and SE ('article?' for 'Article!'—this is an exclamation rather than a question—in I. IV, '*consort,*' for '*Consort*' and '*bird*' for '*Bird!*' in II. XIII, 'distraction' for 'distraction!' in III. XII, and '*friend a*' for '*Friend, a*' in III. XIII). Among the actual errors introduced in TE are '*novissimus*' for '*novimus*' in the epigraph on the title-page, '*Gag*' for '*Gagg*' on the second appearance of the name in I. II, 'injustice!' for 'Injustice?' in II. II, and the assigning of Air XXXI in II. XI to Polly instead of to Lucy. There is also an obvious misprint, '*love*' in Air XIII in I. X, caused by the compositors using '*c*' instead of '*e*'. (What appears to be a similar misprint in some copies, '*werc*' in Air LXVII in III. XIII, is due to a defective '*e*'.) There are very few variants in TE, but in some copies the misprint '*pent*' appears in Air XIII in I. X instead of '*spent*', $F2^v$ and $F3^r$ are incorrectly numbered '24' and '17' respectively instead of '36' and '37', and alternative tailpieces for Acts I (DI^v) and II ($F4^v$) are found. A superficial examination of TE may lead to the conclusion that it is 'more carefully considered' than FE and SE, but a detailed scrutiny reveals that there is very little evidence for this view. The changes introduced in TE that cannot be put down to compositorial carelessness are not consistent with a 'carefully considered' authorial revision, but with an unsystematic and piecemeal attempt by the compositors to regularise the text, an attempt that sometimes produces the opposite of what was intended. I have located twenty-two copies of TE in British libraries: three in the British Museum (79.i.30; Hirsch IV. 1576.(1.); R.M.10.a.6.(1.) in the King's Music Library); two in the National Library of Ireland (Joly Music 5829 and Additional Music 10,925—lacks A1–2); Bodleian Library (Mal. 128(3)); two in the Rowe Music Library, King's College, Cambridge (Rw.83.88A. REF. and Rw.83.88B); Fitzwilliam Museum, Cambridge; London University Library (M782[Gay] / ML Locked Cupboard / For reference only); Music Library, Barber Institute of Fine Arts, Birmingham University (STACK REF. M 1500.B); Reference Library, Birmingham Public Libraries (A782.12—lacks 2G1); Brotherton Collection, Brotherton Library, Leeds University; J. B. Morrell Library, York University (Dyson Collection MA 131.3); Edinburgh University Library (Dm.3.8/1); Central Library, Edinburgh Public Libraries (ANN(9) wMA 491—lacks signature A; signatures H–I between D and E); Glasgow University Library (P.d.14); Mitchell Library, Glasgow (M. Rm.2.6.[2]); St Andrews University Library (Fin M1503.P295); Wighton Music Collection, Dundee Public Libraries (B31980 H); two in the Central Library, Cardiff Public Libraries. Dearing record twelve copies in American libraries: two in Harvard University; three in Yale University; four in the University of Texas; Huntington Library; Library of Congress; Newberry Library.

In addition to collating fifty-six copies of FE, SE and TE, I have examined copies of forty-three editions published after Gay's death in 1732, including most of those issued in the following forty years and most twentieth century editions (see Bibliography). Almost all the eighteenth century editions are based on SE, although a few, such as the two Dublin editions of 1749, derive from FE, like the pirated Dublin editions published before Gay's death. The eighteenth century editions are mainly of interest because they continue the gradual process of regularising Gay's punctuation and spelling begun in some issues of SE and in the pirated editions of 1728.[40] This process was more or less complete by the middle of the century. The earliest edition to dispense with Gay's scene divisions, as a number of twentieth century editions have done, is in the volume of his *Plays* (London, 1760). The neoclassical practice of beginning a new scene every time an important character enters or leaves seems unnecessarily cumbersome today, but since Gay himself adopted it, I have adhered to it in this edition. Few twentieth century editions are based on even a

---

[40] Several non-authorial emendations in SE, especially in SE6–9, are also found, for example, in the Third Dublin Edition (11779.a.15.(1.) in the British Museum and JP 6245 in the National Library of Ireland), and the capitalisation is more consistent in this edition than in FE on which it is based.

modicum of bibliographical and textual analysis. Most derive from TE, and even the best editors, such as G. C. Faber, treat TE with far more respect than it deserves. It is worth noting that twenty-three of the twentieth century editions examined contain an identical error (see Textual Note on II. VII. 18).

Since FE1 was set from Gay's manuscript, I have used one of the well-preserved copies of it (MR.463.c.70.2 in the University Library, Cambridge) as copy-text for this edition, but I have incorporated subsequent additions to and changes in the play-text that are certainly or probably authorial. This means that the extra song and the corrections found in FE5 and all the changes found in SE1 except for the errors introduced during the reimposition and re-setting of the type are included. I have therefore adopted the numbering of the Airs used in SE and in almost all subsequent editions. This system of numbering is more satisfactory than that used in FE because it makes references to the songs unambiguous. The six readings adopted from TE are corrections of minor compositorial errors in FE that are not corrected in SE. Otherwise I have not adopted any of the changes and emendations introduced after SE1 because these are almost certainly not authorial.[41] I have emended the Dramatis Personae at the beginning of II. III, and removed a few speech-prefixes that are unnecessarily repeated at the beginning of scenes, Airs and speeches following Airs. Apart from the numbers of the Airs in Acts II–III, all these departures from the copy-text are recorded in the Textual Notes. When a word is hyphenated over a line-ending in the copy-text in such a way that it could have been hyphenated in Gay's manuscript (e.g. 'Highway-/man's', 'Twelve-/month' and 'Tally-/men'), the form used elsewhere in the text (e.g. 'Highwayman' and 'Twelve-month') or that more usual at the time ('Tally-men') is used. I have added six stage-directions and three speech-prefixes for the sake of clarity, all of which are enclosed in pointed brackets. I have resisted the temptation to introduce numerous stage-directions as some editors have done, because the dialogue makes the action perfectly clear. Most entrances and exits are indicated by the Dramatis Personae at the beginning of scenes. The explanatory note on 'Lock' at the foot of page 95 is Gay's own gloss and

---

[41] It is of course possible that a few 'irregularities' in FE that are retained in SE1, especially commas instead of full-stops, are compositorial errors rather than the readings of Gay's manuscript, but on the other hand Gay's spelling and punctuation are neither consistent nor 'modern', as G. C. Faber has amply documented (*op. cit.*, pp. xvi–xxi), and since the 'irregularities' do not lead to misunderstanding or ambiguity, I have adhered to the copy-text.

is found in FE, SE and TE. As regards the preliminary material, I have expanded the Dramatis Personae at the beginning of the play to include all the minor characters, enclosing the additions in pointed brackets. I have also included 'A TABLE of the SONGS' and 'The Names of the *Lilliputians*', although both of these may well be additions made by the publishers without Gay's authority. The Table of Songs, which does not appear in FE, is based on SE1, but I have adopted a correction found in SE9 and TE, made five emendations for the sake of consistency, and omitted the page references to the original edition. The list of the Lilliputian actors and the parts they played, which does not appear in FE, SE1–4, or TE, is based on SE5, although a correction found in SE6–9 is adopted.

All other departures from the copy-text are of a technical nature and do not affect the text: (i) in the Dramatis Personae at the beginning of the play (but not in the list of Lilliputians, in which the conventions of the original are adhered to) the names of all the characters are printed in roman capitals, MRS being used without a full-stop; (ii) in the stage-directions, speech-prefixes, and Dramatis Personae at the beginning of scenes, the names of individual characters are printed in full in roman capitals (MRS is as above), although POLLY and LUCY rather than POLLY PEACHUM and LUCY LOCKIT are used, as in the copy-text; (iii) in the Paraphernalia, but not in the Text Proper or in the list of Lilliputians, the spelling of MATT (OF THE MINT) is regularised, this being much more usual than the other form found in the copy-text, 'Mat'; (iv) the typography of all headings and the like is regularised, being printed in roman capitals; (v) the contemporary typographical practice of using a full-stop after every heading and the like, including act and scene numbers, as well as after every name in the preliminary lists of characters and actors is abandoned; (vi) at the beginning of each act, the act number is printed above the scene number, and at the beginning of II. VII, III. IV, III. V, and III. VII, the location is printed below the scene number, whereas they occupy the same line in the copy-text; (vii) short 's' is substituted for long 's'; (viii) two separate letters are used instead of ligatures; (ix) the use of roman and italic punctuation and brackets, which is somewhat erratic in the copy-text, is regularised; (x) the abbreviation '*Ex.*' is expanded into '*Exit*'; (xi) the direction '*Aside*' is placed immediately before the words to which it applies, whereas it follows them in the copy-text; (xii) all stage-directions relating to the songs are printed in italics, whereas in the copy-text they are printed in roman type; (xiii) all entrances are ranged left and most other stage-directions are ranged right; (xiv) inessential brackets around stage-directions are omitted; (xv) the rules between scenes are omitted; (xvi) catchwords are not used; (xvii) no attempt has been made to reproduce typographical ornaments. Most of these changes are made silently, but those relating to (x) are recorded in the Textual Notes, as are a few relating to (ii) and (iii) —significant departures from the forms of names given in stage-directions and in the Dramatis Personae at the beginning of scenes, but not from those in speech-prefixes because they are usually abbreviated in the copy-text.

It could be argued that an edition of *The Beggar's Opera* is incomplete without the music, but I have not included the music in this edition for several reasons. Considering the musical superiority of TE, there is little point in reproducing the music of FE or SE, and the excellent photographic reprint of TE can be found in most good libraries. To reproduce the lengthy score of TE would therefore be unnecessarily indulgent, especially in an edition designed primarily for students of drama and literature. Furthermore, if the music is to be included in a critical edition of the play, it too should be edited critically, with variants recorded and with the exact relationship of the tunes to their sources established. This is a task for a musicologist with a good knowledge of the popular music of the early eighteenth century. Potential producers of the play may decide to use one of the modern arrangements, such as those by Frederic Austin (London (Boosey) 1920), Benjamin Britten (London (Boosey and Hawkes) 1949), Edward J. Dent ('45' in the Bibliography), and Edward Smith (in Edgar V. Roberts's edition, '49' in the Bibliography), but many producers would want to adapt the music from TE to suit their own interpretations of the play.

THE

BEGGAR's

OPERA.

As it is Acted at the

THEATRE-ROYAL

IN

LINCOLNS-INN-FIELDS.

Written by Mr. *G A Y.*

————*Nos hæc novimus esse nihil.*   Mart.

To which is Added,

The MUSICK *Engrav'd on* COPPER-PLATES.

L O N D O N:

Printed for J O H N W A T T S, at the Printing-Office
in *Wild-Court,* near *Lincoln's-Inn-Fields.*

MDCCXXVIII.
[Price 1s. 6d.]

Dramatis Personæ.

M E N.

Peachum.	Mr. *Hippesley.*
Lockit.	Mr. *Hall.*
Macheath.	Mr. *Walker.*
Filch.	Mr. *Clark.*
Jemmy Twitcher.	Mr. *H. Bullock.*
Crook-finger'd Jack.	Mr. *Houghton.*
Wat Dreary.	Mr. *Smith.*
Robin *of* Bagshot.	Mr. *Lacy.*
Nimming Ned.	Mr. *Pit.*
Harry Padington,	Mr. *Eaton.*
Mat *of the* Mint.	Mr. *Spiller.*
Ben Budge.	Mr. *Morgan.*
Beggar.	Mr. *Chapman.*
Player.	Mr. *Milward.*

Macheath's Gang. — (Jemmy Twitcher through Ben Budge)

Constables, Drawer, Turnkey, &c.

W O M E N.

Mrs. Peachum	Mrs. *Martin.*
Polly Peachum.	Miss *Fenton.*
Lucy Lockit.	Mrs. *Egleton.*
Diana Trapes.	Mrs. *Martin.*
Mrs. Coaxer.	Mrs. *Holiday*
Dolly Trull.	Mrs. *Lacy.*
Mrs. Vixen.	Mrs. *Rice.*
Betty Doxy.	Mrs. *Rogers.*
Jenny Diver.	Mrs. *Clarke.*
Mrs. Slammekin.	Mrs. *Morgan.*
Suky Tawdry.	Mrs. *Palin.*
Molly Brazen.	Mrs. *Sallee.*

Women of the Town. — (Mrs. Coaxer through Molly Brazen)

A TABLE OF THE SONGS

ACT I

ACT II

ACT III

DRAMATIS PERSONAE

MEN

PEACHUM		Mr. *Hippesley*
LOCKIT		Mr. *Hall*
MACHEATH		Mr. *Walker*
FILCH		Mr. *Clark*
JEMMY TWITCHER		Mr. *H. Bullock*
CROOK-FINGER'D JACK		Mr. *Houghton*
WAT DREARY		Mr. *Smith*
ROBIN OF BAGSHOT	} *Macheath*'s Gang {	Mr. *Lacy*
NIMMING NED		Mr. *Pit*
HARRY PADINGTON		Mr. *Eaton*
MATT OF THE MINT		Mr. *Spiller*
BEN BUDGE		Mr. *Morgan*
BEGGAR		Mr. *Chapman*
PLAYER		Mr. *Milward*

⟨DRAWER, HARPER, SERVANT, JAILOR,
  OTHER MEMBERS OF MACHEATH'S GANG,
  CONSTABLES, TURNKEYS, PRISONERS, RABBLE⟩*

WOMEN

MRS PEACHUM		Mrs. *Martin*
POLLY PEACHUM		Miss *Fenton*
LUCY LOCKIT		Mrs. *Egleton*
DIANA TRAPES		Mrs. *Martin*
MRS COAXER		Mrs. *Holiday*
DOLLY TRULL		Mrs. *Lacy*
MRS VIXEN		Mrs. *Rice*
BETTY DOXY	} *Women of the Town* {	Mrs. *Rogers*
JENNY DIVER		Mrs. *Clarke*
MRS SLAMMEKIN		Mrs. *Morgan*
SUKY TAWDRY		Mrs. *Palin*
MOLLY BRAZEN		Mrs. *Sallee*

⟨FOUR WOMEN AND CHILDREN⟩

---

* DRAWER . . . RABBLE] *Constables, Drawer, Turnkey, &c.* FE, SE, TE.

THE NAMES OF THE LILLIPUTIANS

Mr. Peachum		*Mary Shaftoe*
Lockit		*James Bencraft*
Macheath		*Elizabeth Binks*
Filch		*James Weeks*
Jemmy Twitcher		*Henry Woodward*
Crook-finger'd Jack		*James Weeks*
Wat Dreary		*James Weeks*
Robin *of* Bagshot	*Macheath's* Gang	*John Wilson*
Nimming Ned		*James Bencraft*
Harry Padington		*Fisher Tench Charke*
Mat *of the* Mint		*John Verhuyck*
Ben Budge		*Henry Woodward*
Beggar		*Henry Woodward*
Player		*Fisher Tench Charke*

Constables, Drawer, Turnkey, &c.

Mrs. Peachum		*Esther Wherrit*
Polly Peachum		*Elizabeth Rogers*
Lucy Lockit		*Susanna Rogers*
Diana Trapes		*Esther Wherrit*
Mrs. Coaxer		*Margaret Lowe*
Dolly Trull		*Sarah Foxwell*
Mrs. Vixen		*Mary Vincent*
Betty Doxy	*Women of the Town*	*Mary Weyman*
Jenny Diver		*Margaret Gold*
Mrs. Slammekin		*Esther Wherrit*
Suky Tawdry		*Beatrice Boitar*
Molly Brazen		*Susanna Caun*

INTRODUCTION

BEGGAR. PLAYER.

BEGGAR. If Poverty be a Title to Poetry, I am sure No-body can
dispute mine. I own myself of the Company of Beggars; and I
make one at their Weekly Festivals at St. *Giles*'s. I have a small
Yearly Salary for my Catches, and am welcome to a Dinner there
whenever I please, which is more than most Poets can say.   5
PLAYER. As we live by the Muses, 'tis but Gratitude in us to encourage Poetical Merit where-ever we find it. The Muses, contrary
to all other Ladies, pay no Distinction to Dress, and never partially
mistake the Pertness of Embroidery for Wit, nor the Modesty of
Want for Dulness. Be the Author who he will, we push his Play   10
as far as it will go. So (though you are in Want) I wish you Success
heartily.
BEGGAR. This Piece I own was originally writ for the celebrating
the Marriage of *James Chanter* and *Moll Lay*, two most excellent
Ballad-Singers. I have introduc'd the Similes that are in all your   15
celebrated *Operas*: The *Swallow*, the *Moth*, the *Bee*, the *Ship*, the
Flower, &c. Besides, I have a Prison Scene which the Ladies always
reckon charmingly pathetick. As to the Parts, I have observ'd such
a nice Impartiality to our two Ladies, that it is impossible for
either of them to take Offence. I hope I may be forgiven, that I   20
have not made my Opera throughout unnatural, like those in
vogue; for I have no Recitative: Excepting this, as I have consented to have neither Prologue nor Epilogue, it must be allow'd
an Opera in all its forms. The Piece indeed hath been heretofore
frequently represented by ourselves in our great Room at St. *Giles*'s,   25
so that I cannot too often acknowledge your Charity in bringing
it now on the Stage.
PLAYER. But I see 'tis time for us to withdraw; the Actors are
preparing to begin. Play away the Overture.

Exeunt.

THE BEGGAR'S OPERA

ACT I

SCENE I

SCENE Peachum's *House*.

PEACHUM *sitting at a Table with a large Book of Accounts before him.*

AIR I. An old Woman cloathed in Gray, *&c.*

> *Through all the Employments of Life*
> *Each Neighbour abuses his Brother;*
> *Whore and Rogue they call Husband and Wife:*
> *All Professions be-rogue one another.*
> *The Priest calls the Lawyer a Cheat,*   5
> *The Lawyer be-knaves the Divine;*
> *And the Statesman, because he's so great,*
> *Thinks his Trade as honest as mine.*

A Lawyer is an honest Employment, so is mine. Like me too he
acts in a double Capacity, both against Rogues and for 'em; for   10
'tis but fitting that we should protect and encourage Cheats, since
we live by them.

SCENE II

PEACHUM, FILCH.

FILCH.   Sir, Black *Moll* hath sent word her Tryal comes on in the
Afternoon, and she hopes you will order Matters so as to bring her
off.

PEACHUM.   Why, she may plead her Belly at worst; to my Knowledge she hath taken care of that Security. But as the Wench is   5
very active and industrious, you may satisfy her that I'll soften the
Evidence.

FILCH. *Tom Gagg*, Sir, is found guilty.

PEACHUM. A lazy Dog! When I took him the time before, I told
him what he would come to if he did not mend his Hand. This is   10
Death without Reprieve. I may venture to Book him. [*writes*] For
Tom Gagg, forty Pounds. Let *Betty Sly* know that I'll save her
from Transportation, for I can get more by her staying in *England*.

FILCH. *Betty* hath brought more Goods into our Lock to-year than
any five of the Gang; and in truth, 'tis a pity to lose so good a   15
Customer.

PEACHUM. If none of the Gang take her off, she may, in the
common course of Business, live a Twelve-month longer. I love to
let Women scape. A good Sportsman always lets the Hen Partridges fly, because the breed of the Game depends upon them.   20
Besides, here the Law allows us no Reward; there is nothing to be
got by the Death of Women—except our Wives.

FILCH. Without dispute, she is a fine Woman! 'Twas to her I was
oblig'd for my Education, and (to say a bold Word) she hath
train'd up more young Fellows to the Business than the Gaming-   25
table.

PEACHUM. Truly, *Filch*, thy Observation is right. We and the
Surgeons are more beholden to Women than all the Professions
besides.

AIR 11.   The bonny gray-ey'd Morn, &c.

FILCH. *'Tis Woman that seduces all Mankind,*   30
 By her we first were taught the wheedling Arts:
Her very Eyes can cheat; when most she's kind,
 She tricks us of our Money with our Hearts.
For her, like Wolves by night we roam for Prey,
 And practise ev'ry Fraud to bribe her Charms;   35
For Suits of Love, like Law, are won by Pay,
 And Beauty must be fee'd into our Arms.

PEACHUM. But make haste to *Newgate*, Boy, and let my Friends
know what I intend; for I love to make them easy one way or other.

FILCH. When a Gentleman is long kept in suspence, Penitence   40
may break his Spirit ever after. Besides, Certainty gives a Man a
good Air upon his Tryal, and makes him risque another without
Fear or Scruple. But I'll away, for 'tis a Pleasure to be the Messen-
ger of Comfort to Friends in Affliction.

SCENE III

PEACHUM.

But 'tis now high time to look about me for a decent Execution against next Sessions. I hate a lazy Rogue, by whom one can get nothing 'till he is hang'd. A Register of the Gang, [*reading*] Crook-finger'd *Jack*. A Year and a half in the Service; Let me see how much the Stock owes to his Industry; one, two, three, four, five 5 Gold Watches, and seven Silver ones. A mighty clean-handed Fellow! Sixteen Snuff-boxes, five of them of true Gold. Six dozen of Handkerchiefs, four silver-hilted Swords, half a dozen of Shirts, three Tye-Perriwigs, and a Piece of Broad Cloth. Considering these are only the Fruits of his leisure Hours, I don't know a 10 prettier Fellow, for no Man alive hath a more engaging Presence of Mind upon the Road. *Wat Dreary*, alias *Brown Will*, an irregular Dog, who hath an underhand way of disposing of his Goods. I'll try him only for a Sessions or two longer upon his good Behaviour. *Harry Padington*, a poor petty-larceny Rascal, without the least 15 Genius; that Fellow, though he were to live these six Months, will never come to the Gallows with any Credit. Slippery *Sam*; he goes off the next Sessions, for the Villain hath the Impudence to have views of following his Trade as a Taylor, which he calls an honest Employment. *Mat* of the *Mint*; listed not above a Month 20 ago, a promising sturdy Fellow, and diligent in his way; somewhat too bold and hasty, and may raise good Contributions on the Publick, if he does not cut himself short by Murder. *Tom. Tipple*, a guzzling soaking Sot, who is always too drunk to stand himself, or to make others stand. A Cart is absolutely necessary for him. 25 *Robin* of *Bagshot*, alias *Gorgon*, alias *Bluff Bob*, alias *Carbuncle*, alias *Bob Booty*.

SCENE IV

PEACHUM, MRS PEACHUM.

MRS PEACHUM.   What of *Bob Booty*, Husband? I hope nothing bad hath betided him. You know, my Dear, he's a favourite Customer of mine. 'Twas he made me a Present of this Ring.
PEACHUM.   I have set his Name down in the Black-List, that's all,

my Dear; he spends his Life among Women, and as soon as his   5
Money is gone, one or other of the Ladies will hang him for the
Reward, and there's forty Pound lost to us for-ever.

MRS PEACHUM.   You know, my Dear, I never meddle in matters
of Death; I always leave those Affairs to you. Women indeed are
bitter bad Judges in these cases, for they are so partial to the Brave   10
that they think every Man handsome who is going to the Camp or
the Gallows.

AIR III.   Cold and Raw, &c.

If any Wench Venus's *Girdle wear,*
    Though she be never so ugly;
Lillys and Roses will quickly appear,   15
    And her Face look wond'rous smuggly.
Beneath the left Ear so fit but a Cord,
    (A Rope so charming a Zone is!)
The Youth in his Cart hath the Air of a Lord,
    And we cry, There dies an Adonis!   20

But really, Husband, you should not be too hard-hearted, for you
never had a finer, braver set of Men than at present. We have not
had a Murder among them all, these seven Months. And truly, my
Dear, that is a great Blessing.

PEACHUM.   What a dickens is the Woman always a whimpring   25
about Murder for? No Gentleman is ever look'd upon the worse
for killing a Man in his own Defence; and if Business cannot be
carried on without it, what would you have a Gentleman do?

MRS PEACHUM.   If I am in the wrong, my Dear, you must
excuse me, for No-body can help the Frailty of an over-scrupulous   30
Conscience.

PEACHUM.   Murder is as fashionable a Crime as a Man can be guilty
of. How many fine Gentlemen have we in *Newgate* every Year,
purely upon that Article! If they have wherewithal to persuade the
Jury to bring it in Manslaughter, what are they the worse for it?   35
So, my Dear, have done upon this Subject. Was Captain *Macheath*
here this Morning, for the Bank-notes he left with you last Week?

MRS PEACHUM.   Yes, my Dear; and though the Bank hath stopt
Payment, he was so cheerful and so agreeable! Sure there is not a
finer Gentleman upon the Road than the Captain! If he comes   40

from *Bagshot* at any reasonable Hour he hath promis'd to make one
this Evening with *Polly* and me, and *Bob Booty*, at a Party of
Quadrille. Pray, my Dear, is the Captain rich?

PEACHUM.   The Captain keeps too good Company ever to grow
rich. *Mary-bone* and the Chocolate-houses are his undoing. The   45
Man that proposes to get Money by Play should have the Education
of a fine Gentleman, and be train'd up to it from his Youth.

MRS PEACHUM.   Really, I am sorry upon *Polly*'s Account the
Captain hath not more Discretion. What business hath he to keep
Company with Lords and Gentlemen? he should leave them to   50
prey upon one another.

PEACHUM.   Upon *Polly*'s Account! What, a Plague, does the
Woman mean?—Upon *Polly*'s Account!

MRS PEACHUM.   Captain *Macheath* is very fond of the Girl.

PEACHUM.   And what then?   55

MRS PEACHUM.   If I have any Skill in the Ways of Women, I am
sure *Polly* thinks him a very pretty Man.

PEACHUM.   And what then? You would not be so mad to have the
Wench marry him! Gamesters and Highwaymen are generally very
good to their Whores, but they are very Devils to their Wives.   60

MRS PEACHUM.   But if *Polly* should be in love, how should we help
her, or how can she help herself? Poor Girl, I am in the utmost
Concern about her.

AIR IV.   Why is your faithful Slave disdain'd? &c.

> *If Love the Virgin's Heart invade,*
> *How, like a Moth, the simple Maid*   65
>   *Still plays about the Flame!*
> *If soon she be not made a Wife,*
> *Her Honour's sing'd, and then for Life,*
>   *She's—what I dare not name.*

PEACHUM.   Look ye, Wife. A handsome Wench in our way of   70
Business is as profitable as at the Bar of a *Temple* Coffee-House,
who looks upon it as her Livelihood to grant every Liberty but
one. You see I would indulge the Girl as far as prudently we can.
In any thing, but Marriage! After that, my Dear, how shall we be
safe? Are we not then in her Husband's Power? For a Husband   75
hath the absolute Power over all a Wife's Secrets but her own. If

the Girl had the Discretion of a Court Lady, who can have a dozen young Fellows at her Ear without complying with one, I should not matter it; but *Polly* is Tinder, and a Spark will at once set her on a Flame. Married! If the Wench does not know her own Profit, sure she knows her own Pleasure better than to make herself a Property! My Daughter to me should be, like a Court Lady to a Minister of State, a Key to the whole Gang. Married! If the Affair is not already done, I'll terrify her from it, by the Example of our Neighbours.

MRS PEACHUM. May-hap, my Dear, you may injure the Girl. She loves to imitate the fine Ladies, and she may only allow the Captain Liberties in the View of Interest.

PEACHUM. But 'tis your Duty, my Dear, to warn the Girl against her Ruin, and to instruct her how to make the most of her Beauty. I'll go to her this moment, and sift her. In the mean time, Wife, rip out the Coronets and Marks of these dozen of Cambric Handkerchiefs, for I can dispose of them this Afternoon to a Chap in the City.

SCENE V

MRS PEACHUM.

Never was a Man more out of the way in an Argument than my Husband! Why must our *Polly*, forsooth, differ from her Sex, and love only her Husband? And why must *Polly*'s Marriage, contrary to all Observation, make her the less followed by other Men? All Men are Thieves in Love, and like a Woman the better for being another's Property.

AIR V. Of all the simple Things we do, &c.

A Maid is like the golden Oar,
Which hath Guineas intrinsical in't,
Whose Worth is never known, before
It is try'd and imprest in the Mint.
A Wife's like a Guinea in Gold,
Stampt with the Name of her Spouse;
Now here, now there; is bought, or is sold;
And is current in every House.

SCENE VI

MRS PEACHUM, FILCH.

MRS PEACHUM.   Come hither *Filch*. I am as fond of this Child, as
though my Mind misgave me he were my own. He hath as fine a
Hand at picking a Pocket as a Woman, and is as nimble-finger'd
as a Juggler. If an unlucky Session does not cut the Rope of thy
Life, I pronounce, Boy, thou wilt be a great Man in History.   5
Where was your Post last Night, my Boy?

FILCH.   I ply'd at the Opera, Madam; and considering 'twas neither
dark nor rainy, so that there was no great Hurry in getting Chairs
and Coaches, made a tolerable hand on't. These seven Handkerchiefs, Madam.   10

MRS PEACHUM.   Colour'd ones, I see. They are of sure Sale from
our Ware-house at *Redriff* among the Seamen.

FILCH.   And this Snuff-box.

MRS PEACHUM.   Set in Gold! A pretty Encouragement this to a
young Beginner.   15

FILCH.   I had a fair tug at a charming Gold Watch. Pox take the
Taylors for making the Fobs so deep and narrow! It stuck by the
way, and I was forc'd to make my Escape under a Coach. Really,
Madam, I fear I shall be cut off in the Flower of my Youth, so that
every now and then (since I was pumpt) I have thoughts of taking 20
up and going to Sea.

MRS PEACHUM.   You should go to *Hockley in the Hole*, and to
Marybone, Child, to learn Valour. These are the Schools that have
bred so many brave Men. I thought, Boy, by this time, thou hadst
lost Fear as well as Shame. Poor Lad! how little does he know as   25
yet of the *Old-Baily*! For the first Fact I'll insure thee from being
hang'd; and going to Sea, *Filch*, will come time enough upon a Sentence of Transportation. But now, since you have nothing better
to do, ev'n go to your Book, and learn your Catechism; for really a
Man makes but an ill Figure in the Ordinary's Paper, who cannot   30
give a satisfactory Answer to his Questions. But, hark you, my Lad.
Don't tell me a Lye; for you know I hate a Lyar. Do you know of
any thing that hath past between Captain *Macheath* and our
Polly?

FILCH.   I beg you, Madam, don't ask me; for I must either tell a Lye   35
to you or to Miss *Polly*; for I promis'd her I would not tell.

C

Mrs Peachum. But when the Honour of our Family is concern'd —

Filch. I shall lead a sad Life with Miss *Polly*, if ever she come to
know that I told you. Besides, I would not willingly forfeit my own   40
Honour by betraying any body.

Mrs Peachum. Yonder comes my Husband and *Polly*. Come,
Filch, you shall go with me into my own Room, and tell me the
whole Story. I'll give thee a Glass of a most delicious Cordial that I
keep for my own drinking.   45

SCENE VII

Peachum, Polly.

Polly. I know as well as any of the fine Ladies how to make the
most of my self and of my Man too. A Woman knows how to be
mercenary, though she hath never been in a Court or at an Assembly. We have it in our Natures, Papa. If I allow Captain *Macheath*
some trifling Liberties, I have this Watch and other visible Marks   5
of his Favour to show for it. A Girl who cannot grant some Things,
and refuse what is most material, will make but a poor hand of her
Beauty, and soon be thrown upon the Common.

AIR VI. What shall I do to show how much I love her, *&c.*

> *Virgins are like the fair Flower in its Lustre,*
> *Which in the Garden enamels the Ground;*   10
> *Near it the Bees in Play flutter and cluster,*
> *And gaudy Butterflies frolick around.*
> *But, when once pluck'd, 'tis no longer alluring,*
> *To* Covent-Garden *'tis sent, (as yet sweet,)*
> *There fades, and shrinks, and grows past all enduring,*   15
> *Rots, stinks, and dies, and is trod under feet.*

Peachum. You know, *Polly*, I am not against your toying and
trifling with a Customer in the way of Business, or to get out a
Secret, or so. But if I find out that you have play'd the fool and are
married, you Jade you, I'll cut your Throat, Hussy. Now you   20
know my Mind.

SCENE VIII

PEACHUM, POLLY, MRS PEACHUM.

AIR VII. Oh *London* is a fine Town.

MRS PEACHUM, *in a very great Passion.*

> *Our* Polly *is a sad Slut! nor heeds what we have taught her.*
> *I wonder any Man alive will ever rear a Daughter!*
> *For she must have both Hoods and Gowns, and Hoops to swell her*
>   *Pride,*
> *With Scarfs and Stays, and Gloves and Lace; and she will have*
>   *Men beside;*
> *And when she's drest with Care and Cost, all-tempting, fine and*
>   *gay,*   5
> *As Men should serve a Cowcumber, she flings herself away.*
> *Our* Polly *is a sad Slut,* &c.

You Baggage! you Hussy! you inconsiderate Jade! had you been
hang'd, it would not have vex'd me, for that might have been your
Misfortune; but to do such a mad thing by Choice! The Wench is   10
married, Husband.

PEACHUM. Married! The Captain is a bold Man, and will risque
any thing for Money; to be sure he believes her a Fortune. Do you
think your Mother and I should have liv'd comfortably so long
together, if ever we had been married? Baggage!   15

MRS PEACHUM. I knew she was always a proud Slut; and now the
Wench hath play'd the Fool and married, because forsooth she
would do like the Gentry. Can you support the Expence of a
Husband, Hussy, in gaming, drinking and whoring? have you
Money enough to carry on the daily Quarrels of Man and Wife   20
about who shall squander most? There are not many Husbands and
Wives, who can bear the Charges of plaguing one another in a
handsome way. If you must be married, could you introduce
no-body into our Family but a Highwayman? Why, thou
foolish Jade, thou wilt be as ill-us'd, and as much neglected, as if   25
thou hadst married a Lord!

PEACHUM. Let not your Anger, my Dear, break through the
Rules of Decency, for the Captain looks upon himself in the

Military Capacity, as a Gentleman by his Profession. Besides what he hath already, I know he is in a fair way of getting, or of dying; 30 and both these ways, let me tell you, are most excellent Chances for a Wife. Tell me Hussy, are you ruin'd or no?

MRS PEACHUM. With *Polly*'s Fortune, she might very well have gone off to a Person of Distinction. Yes, that you might, you pouting Slut! 35

PEACHUM. What, is the Wench dumb? Speak, or I'll make you plead by squeezing out an Answer from you. Are you really bound Wife to him, or are you only upon liking?

Pinches her.

POLLY. Oh! [*Screaming.*]

MRS PEACHUM. How the Mother is to be pitied who hath hand- 40 some Daughters! Locks, Bolts, Bars, and Lectures of Morality are nothing to them: They break through them all. They have as much Pleasure in cheating a Father and Mother, as in cheating at Cards.

PEACHUM. Why, *Polly*, I shall soon know if you are married, by 45 *Macheath*'s keeping from our House.

AIR VIII.   Grim King of the Ghosts, &c.

POLLY. *Can Love be controul'd by Advice?*
Will Cupid *our Mothers obey?*
Though my Heart were as frozen as Ice,
At his Flame 'twould have melted away. 50

When he kist me so closely he prest,
'Twas so sweet that I must have comply'd:
So I thought it both safest and best
To marry, for fear you should chide.

MRS PEACHUM. Then all the Hopes of our Family are gone for 55 ever and ever!

PEACHUM. And *Macheath* may hang his Father and Mother-in-Law, in hope to get into their Daughter's Fortune.

POLLY. I did not marry him (as 'tis the Fashion) cooly and deliberately for Honour or Money. But, I love him. 60

MRS PEACHUM.   Love him! worse and worse! I thought the Girl
had been better bred. Oh Husband, Husband! her Folly makes me
mad! my Head swims! I'm distracted! I can't support myself—Oh!

Faints.

PEACHUM.   See, Wench, to what a Condition you have reduc'd
your poor Mother! a Glass of Cordial, this instant. How the poor   65
Woman takes it to Heart!

POLLY *goes out, and returns with it.*

Ah, Hussy, now this is the only Comfort your Mother has left!
POLLY.   Give her another Glass, Sir; my Mama drinks double the
Quantity whenever she is out of Order. This, you see, fetches her.
MRS PEACHUM.   The Girl shows such a Readiness, and so much   70
Concern, that I could almost find in my Heart to forgive her.

AIR IX.   O *Jenny*, O *Jenny*, where hast thou been.

> O Polly, *you might have toy'd and kist.*
> *By keeping Men off, you keep them on.*
POLLY.   *But he so teaz'd me,*
> *And he so pleas'd me,*   75
> *What I did, you must have done.*

MRS PEACHUM.   Not with a Highwayman.—You sorry Slut!
PEACHUM.   A Word with you, Wife. 'Tis no new thing for a
Wench to take Man without consent of Parents. You know 'tis the
Frailty of Woman, my Dear.   80
MRS PEACHUM.   Yes, indeed, the Sex is frail. But the first time a
Woman is frail, she should be somewhat nice methinks, for then
or never is the time to make her Fortune. After that, she hath
nothing to do but to guard herself from being found out, and she
may do what she pleases.   85
PEACHUM.   Make your self a little easy; I have a Thought shall
soon set all Matters again to rights. Why so melancholy, *Polly?*
since what is done cannot be undone, we must all endeavour to
make the best of it.
MRS PEACHUM.   Well, *Polly*; as far as one Woman can forgive   90
another, I forgive thee.—Your Father is too fond of you, Hussy.
POLLY.   Then all my Sorrows are at an end.

MRS PEACHUM.   A mighty likely Speech in troth, for a Wench who is just married!

AIR X.   *Thomas, I cannot, &c.*

POLLY.   *I, like a Ship in Storms, was tost;*   95
Yet afraid to put in to Land;
For seiz'd in the Port the Vessel's lost,
Whose Treasure is contreband.
   The Waves are laid,
   My Duty's paid.   100
O Joy beyond Expression!
   Thus, safe a-shore,
   I ask no more,
My All is in my Possession.

PEACHUM.   I hear Customers in t'other Room; Go, talk with 'em, 105 *Polly*; but come to us again, as soon as they are gone.—But, heark ye, Child, if 'tis the Gentleman who was here Yesterday about the Repeating-Watch; say, you believe we can't get Intelligence of it, till to-morrow. For I lent it to *Suky Straddle*, to make a Figure with it to-night at a Tavern in *Drury-Lane.* If t'other Gentleman calls 110 for the Silver-hilted Sword; you know Beetle-brow'd *Jemmy* hath it on, and he doth not come from *Tunbridge* till *Tuesday* Night; so that it cannot be had till then.

SCENE IX

PEACHUM, MRS PEACHUM.

PEACHUM.   Dear Wife, be a little pacified. Don't let your Passion run away with your Senses. *Polly*, I grant you, hath done a rash thing.

MRS PEACHUM.   If she had had only an Intrigue with the Fellow, why the very best Families have excus'd and huddled up a Frailty 5 of that sort. 'Tis Marriage, Husband, that makes it a Blemish.

PEACHUM.   But Money, Wife, is the true Fuller's Earth for Reputations, there is not a Spot or a Stain but what it can take out. A rich Rogue now-a-days is fit Company for any Gentleman; and the World, my Dear, hath not such a Contempt for Roguery as you 10 imagine. I tell you, Wife, I can make this Match turn to our Advantage.

MRS PEACHUM. I am very sensible, Husband, that Captain *Macheath* is worth Money, but I am in doubt whether he hath not two or three Wives already, and then if he should dye in a Session or two, *Polly*'s Dower would come into Dispute.   15

PEACHUM. That, indeed, is a Point which ought to be consider'd.

AIR XI.   A Soldier and a Sailor.

> *A Fox may steal your Hens, Sir,*
> *A Whore your Health and Pence, Sir,*
> *Your Daughter rob your Chest, Sir,*   20
> *Your Wife may steal your Rest, Sir,*
>   *A Thief your Goods and Plate.*
> *But this is all but picking,*
> *With Rest, Pence, Chest and Chicken;*
> *It ever was decreed, Sir,*   25
> *If Lawyer's Hand is fee'd, Sir,*
>   *He steals your whole Estate.*

The Lawyers are bitter Enemies to those in our Way. They don't care that any Body should get a Clandestine Livelihood but themselves.   30

SCENE X

MRS PEACHUM, PEACHUM, POLLY.

POLLY. 'Twas only Nimming *Ned*. He brought in a Damask Window-Curtain, a Hoop-Petticoat, a Pair of Silver Candlesticks, a Perriwig, and one Silk Stocking, from the Fire that happen'd last Night.

PEACHUM. There is not a Fellow that is cleverer in his way, and saves more Goods out of the Fire than *Ned*. But now, *Polly*, to your Affair; for Matters must not be left as they are. You are married then, it seems?   5

POLLY. Yes, Sir.

PEACHUM. And how do you propose to live, Child?   10

POLLY. Like other Women, Sir, upon the Industry of my Husband.

MRS PEACHUM. What, is the Wench turn'd Fool? A Highwayman's Wife, like a Soldier's, hath as little of his Pay, as of his
Company.

PEACHUM.   And had not you the common Views of a Gentlewoman   15
in your Marriage, *Polly*?

POLLY.   I don't know what you mean, Sir.

PEACHUM.   Of a Jointure, and of being a Widow.

POLLY.   But I love him, Sir: how then could I have Thoughts of
parting with him?   20

PEACHUM.   Parting with him! Why, that is the whole Scheme and
Intention of all Marriage Articles. The comfortable Estate of
Widow-hood, is the only Hope that keeps up a Wife's Spirits.
Where is the Woman who would scruple to be a Wife, if she had it
in her Power to be a Widow whenever she pleas'd? If you have   25
any Views of this sort, *Polly*, I shall think the Match not so very
unreasonable.

POLLY.   How I dread to hear your Advice! Yet I must beg you to
explain yourself.

PEACHUM.   Secure what he hath got, have him peach'd the next   30
Sessions, and then at once you are made a rich Widow.

POLLY.   What, murder the Man I love! The Blood runs cold at my
Heart with the very Thought of it.

PEACHUM.   Fye, *Polly*! What hath Murder to do in the Affair?
Since the thing sooner or later must happen, I dare say, the   35
Captain himself would like that we should get the Reward for his
Death sooner than a Stranger. Why, *Polly*, the Captain knows,
that as 'tis his Employment to rob, so 'tis ours to take Robbers;
every Man in his Business. So that there is no Malice in the Case.

MRS PEACHUM.   Ay, Husband, now you have nick'd the Matter.   40
To have him peach'd is the only thing could ever make me forgive
her.

AIR XII.   Now ponder well, ye Parents dear.

POLLY.   *Oh, ponder well! be not severe;*
            So save a wretched Wife!
            For on the Rope that hangs my Dear   45
                Depends poor Polly's *Life.*

MRS PEACHUM. But your Duty to your Parents, Hussy, obliges you to hang him. What would many a Wife give for such an Opportunity!

POLLY. What is a Jointure, what is Widow-hood to me? I know my Heart. I cannot survive him.

AIR XIII.   Le printemps rappelle aux armes.

The Turtle thus with plaintive crying,
Her Lover dying,
The Turtle thus with plaintive crying,
Laments her Dove.
Down she drops quite spent with sighing,
Pair'd in Death, as pair'd in Love.

Thus, Sir, it will happen to your poor *Polly.*

MRS PEACHUM.   What, is the Fool in Love in earnest then? I hate thee for being particular: Why, Wench, thou art a Shame to thy very Sex.

POLLY.   But hear me, Mother.—If you ever lov'd —

MRS PEACHUM.   Those cursed Play-books she reads have been her Ruin. One Word more, Hussy, and I shall knock your Brains out, if you have any.

PEACHUM.   Keep out of the way, *Polly,* for fear of Mischief, and consider of what is propos'd to you.

MRS PEACHUM. Away, Hussy. Hang your Husband, and be dutiful.

SCENE XI

MRS PEACHUM, PEACHUM.

POLLY *listning.*

MRS PEACHUM.   The Thing, Husband, must and shall be done. For the sake of Intelligence we must take other Measures, and have him peach'd the next Session without her Consent. If she will not know her Duty, we know ours.

PEACHUM.   But really, my Dear, it grieves one's Heart to take off a   5
great Man. When I consider his Personal Bravery, his fine Strata-
gem, how much we have already got by him, and how much more
we may get, methinks I can't find in my Heart to have a Hand in his
Death. I wish you could have made *Polly* undertake it.

MRS PEACHUM.   But in a Case of Necessity—our own Lives are in   10
danger.

PEACHUM.   Then, indeed, we must comply with the Customs of
the World, and make Gratitude give way to Interest.—He shall be
taken off.

MRS PEACHUM.   I'll undertake to manage *Polly*.   15

PEACHUM.   And I'll prepare Matters for the *Old-Baily*.

SCENE XII

POLLY.

Now I'm a Wretch, indeed.—Methinks I see him already in the Cart,
sweeter and more lovely than the Nosegay in his Hand!—I hear the
Crowd extolling his Resolution and Intrepidity!—What Vollies
of Sighs are sent from the Windows of *Holborn*, that so comely a
Youth should be brought to disgrace!—I see him at the Tree! The   5
whole Circle are in Tears!—even Butchers weep!—*Jack Ketch*
himself hesitates to perform his Duty, and would be glad to lose
his Fee, by a Reprieve. What then will become of *Polly*!—As yet
I may inform him of their Design, and aid him in his Escape.—It
shall be so.—But then he flies, absents himself, and I bar my self   10
from his dear dear Conversation! That too will distract me.—If he
keep out of the way, my Papa and Mama may in time relent, and
we may be happy.—If he stays, he is hang'd, and then he is lost
for ever!—He intended to lye conceal'd in my Room, 'till the Dusk
of the Evening: If they are abroad, I'll this Instant let him out, lest   15
some Accident should prevent him.

Exit, and returns.

SCENE XIII
POLLY, MACHEATH.

AIR XIV.   Pretty Parrot, say —

MACHEATH. *Pretty Polly, say,*
When I was away,
Did your Fancy never stray
To some newer Lover?
POLLY. *Without Disguise,*   5
Heaving Sighs,
Doating Eyes,
My constant Heart discover.
Fondly let me loll!
MACHEATH. *O pretty, pretty Poll.*   10

POLLY.   And are *you* as fond as ever, my Dear?
MACHEATH.   Suspect my Honour, my Courage, suspect any thing
but my Love.—May my Pistols miss Fire, and my Mare slip her
Shoulder while I am pursu'd, if I ever forsake thee!
POLLY.   Nay, my Dear, I have no Reason to doubt you, for I find in | 15
the Romance you lent me, none of the great Heroes were ever false
in Love.

AIR XV.   Pray, Fair One, be kind —

MACHEATH. *My Heart was so free,*
It rov'd like the Bee,
'Till Polly my Passion requited;   20
I sipt each Flower,
I chang'd ev'ry Hour,
But here ev'ry Flower is united.

POLLY.   Were you sentenc'd to Transportation, sure, my Dear,
you could not leave me behind you—could you?   25
MACHEATH.   Is there any Power, any Force that could tear me
from thee? You might sooner tear a Pension out of the Hands of a
Courtier, a Fee from a Lawyer, a pretty Woman from a Looking-
glass, or any Woman from *Quadrille.*—But to tear me from thee is
impossible!   30

AIR XVI.   Over the Hills and far away.

> *Were I laid on* Greenland's *Coast,*
> *And in my Arms embrac'd my Lass;*
> *Warm amidst eternal Frost,*
> *Too soon the Half Year's Night would pass.*

POLLY.　　*Were I sold on* Indian *Soil,*　　　　　　　35
> *Soon as the burning Day was clos'd,*
> *I could mock the sultry Toil,*
> *When on my Charmer's Breast repos'd.*

MACHEATH.　*And I would love you all the Day,*

POLLY.　　*Every Night would kiss and play,*　　　　40

MACHEATH.　*If with me you'd fondly stray*

POLLY.　　*Over the Hills and far away.*

Yes, I would go with thee. But oh!—how shall I speak it? I must
be torn from thee. We must part.

MACHEATH.   How! Part!　　　　　　　　　　　　45

POLLY.   We must, we must.—My Papa and Mama are set against
thy Life. They now, even now are in Search after thee. They
are preparing Evidence against thee. Thy Life depends upon
a Moment.

AIR XVII.   Gin thou wert mine awn thing —

> *O what Pain it is to part!*　　　　　　　　　50
> *Can I leave thee, can I leave thee?*
> *O what Pain it is to part!*
> *Can thy* Polly *ever leave thee?*
> *But lest Death my Love should thwart,*
> *And bring thee to the fatal Cart,*　　　　　55
> *Thus I tear thee from my bleeding Heart!*
> 　*Fly hence, and let me leave thee.*

One Kiss and then—one Kiss—begone—farewell.

MACHEATH.   My Hand, my Heart, my Dear, is so rivited to thine,
that I cannot unloose my Hold.　　　　　　　　　60

POLLY.   But my Papa may intercept thee, and then I should lose
the very glimmering of Hope. A few Weeks, perhaps, may reconcile us all. Shall thy *Polly* hear from thee?

MACHEATH.   Must I then go?

POLLY.   And will not Absence change your Love?   65
MACHEATH.   If you doubt it, let me stay—and be hang'd.
POLLY.   O how I fear! how I tremble!—Go—but when Safety will
   give you leave, you will be sure to see me again; for 'till then *Polly*
   is wretched.

AIR XVIII.   O the Broom, &c.

*[Parting, and looking back at each other with
fondness; he at one Door, she at the other.*

MACHEATH.   *The Miser thus a Shilling sees,*   70
                   Which he's oblig'd to pay,
                   With Sighs resigns it by degrees,
                   And fears 'tis gone for aye.

POLLY.   *The Boy, thus, when his Sparrow's flown,*
                   The Bird in Silence eyes;   75
                   But soon as out of Sight 'tis gone,
                   Whines, whimpers, sobs and cries.

ACT II

SCENE I

A Tavern near Newgate.

JEMMY TWITCHER, CROOK-FINGER'D JACK, WAT DREARY, ROBIN OF BAGSHOT, NIMMING NED, HENRY PADINGTON, MATT OF THE MINT, BEN BUDGE, *and the rest of the Gang, at the Table, with Wine, Brandy and Tobacco.*

BEN BUDGE.   But pr'ythee, *Matt*, what is become of thy Brother *Tom?* I have not seen him since my Return from Transportation.

MATT OF THE MINT.   Poor Brother *Tom* had an Accident this time Twelve-month, and so clever a made Fellow he was, that I could not save him from those fleaing Rascals the Surgeons; and now,   5 poor Man, he is among the Otamys at *Surgeon's Hall.*

BEN BUDGE.   So it seems, his Time was come.

JEMMY TWITCHER.   But the present Time is ours, and no Body alive hath more. Why are the Laws levell'd at us? are we more dishonest than the rest of Mankind? What we win, Gentlemen, is   10 our own by the Law of Arms, and the Right of Conquest.

CROOK-FINGER'D JACK.   Where shall we find such another Set of practical Philosophers, who to a Man are above the Fear of Death?

WAT DREARY.   Sound Men, and true!   15

ROBIN OF BAGSHOT.   Of try'd Courage, and indefatigable Industry!

NIMMING NED.   Who is there here that would not dye for his Friend?

HARRY PADINGTON.   Who is there here that would betray him   20 for his Interest?

MATT OF THE MINT.   Show me a Gang of Courtiers that can say as much.

BEN BUDGE.   We are for a just Partition of the World, for every Man hath a Right to enjoy Life.   25

MATT OF THE MINT.   We retrench the Superfluities of Mankind. The World is avaritious, and I hate Avarice. A covetous fellow,

like a Jack-daw, steals what he was never made to enjoy, for the sake of hiding it. These are the Robbers of Mankind, for Money was made for the Free-hearted and Generous, and where is the   30
Injury of taking from another, what he hath not the Heart to make use of?

JEMMY TWITCHER.   Our several Stations for the Day are fixt. Good luck attend us all. Fill the Glasses.

AIR XIX.   Fill ev'ry Glass, &c.

MATT OF THE MINT.
>   *Fill ev'ry Glass, for Wine inspires us,*   35
>   *And fires us*
>   *With Courage, Love and Joy.*
>   *Women and Wine should Life employ.*
>   *Is there ought else on Earth desirous?*
CHORUS.   *Fill ev'ry Glass*, &c.   40

SCENE II

To them enter MACHEATH.

MACHEATH.   Gentlemen, well met. My Heart hath been with you this Hour; but an unexpected Affair hath detain'd me. No Ceremony, I beg you.

MATT OF THE MINT.   We were just breaking up to go upon Duty. Am I to have the Honour of taking the Air with you, Sir,   5
this Evening upon the Heath? I drink a Dram now and then with the Stage-Coachmen in the way of Friendship and Intelligence; and I know that about this Time there will be Passengers upon the Western Road, who are worth speaking with.

MACHEATH.   I was to have been of that Party—but —   10

MATT OF THE MINT.   But what, Sir?

MACHEATH.   Is there any man who suspects my Courage?

MATT OF THE MINT.   We have all been witnesses of it.

MACHEATH.   My Honour and Truth to the Gang?

MATT OF THE MINT.   I'll be answerable for it.   15

MACHEATH.   In the Division of our Booty, have I ever shown the least Marks of Avarice or Injustice?

MATT OF THE MINT.   By these Questions something seems to have ruffled you. Are any of us suspected?

MACHEATH.   I have a fixt Confidence, Gentlemen, in you all, as   20
Men of Honour, and as such I value and respect you. *Peachum* is a
Man that is useful to us.

MATT OF THE MINT.   Is he about to play us any foul Play? I'll
shoot him through the Head.

MACHEATH.   I beg you, Gentlemen, act with Conduct and Dis-   25
cretion. A Pistol is your last resort.

MATT OF THE MINT.   He knows nothing of this Meeting.

MACHEATH.   Business cannot go on without him. He is a Man who
knows the World, and is a necessary Agent to us. We have had a
slight Difference, and till it is accommodated I shall be oblig'd to   30
keep out of his way. Any private Dispute of mine shall be of no ill
consequence to my Friends. You must continue to act under his
Direction, for the moment we break loose from him, our Gang is
ruin'd.

MATT OF THE MINT.   As a Bawd to a Whore, I grant you, he is to   35
us of great Convenience.

MACHEATH.   Make him believe I have quitted the Gang, which I
can never do but with Life. At our private Quarters I will continue
to meet you. A Week or so will probably reconcile us.

MATT OF THE MINT.   Your Instructions shall be observ'd. 'Tis   40
now high time for us to repair to our several Duties; so till the
Evening at our Quarters in *Moor-fields* we bid you farewell.

MACHEATH.   I shall wish my self with you. Success attend you.

Sits down melancholy at the Table.

AIR XX.   March in *Rinaldo*, with Drums and Trumpets.

MATT OF THE MINT.
        Let us take the Road.
          Hark! I hear the sound of Coaches!   45
          The hour of Attack approaches,
      To your Arms, brave Boys, and load.
          See the Ball I hold!
          Let the Chymists toil like Asses,
          Our Fire their Fire surpasses,   50
          And turns all our Lead to Gold.

*The Gang, rang'd in the Front of the Stage, load their Pistols, and stick
them under their Girdles; then go off singing the first Part in Chorus.*

SCENE III

MACHEATH.

What a Fool is a fond Wench! *Polly* is most confoundedly bit.—I
love the Sex. And a Man who loves Money, might as well be con-
tented with one Guinea, as I with one Woman. The Town perhaps
hath been as much oblig'd to me, for recruiting it with free-
hearted Ladies, as to any Recruiting Officer in the Army. If it   5
were not for us and the other Gentlemen of the Sword, *Drury-
Lane* would be uninhabited.

AIR XXI.   Would you have a Young Virgin, *&c.*

If the Heart of a Man is deprest with Cares,
The Mist is dispell'd when a Woman appears;
Like the Notes of a Fiddle, she sweetly, sweetly   10
Raises the Spirits, and charms our Ears,
   Roses and Lillies her Cheeks disclose,
   But her ripe Lips are more sweet than those.
     Press her,
     Caress her   15
     With Blisses,
     Her Kisses
Dissolve us in Pleasure, and soft Repose.

I must have Women. There is nothing unbends the Mind like them.
Money is not so strong a Cordial for the Time. Drawer. —   20

Enter DRAWER.

Is the Porter gone for all the Ladies, according to my directions?
DRAWER.   I expect him back every Minute. But you know, Sir, you
sent him as far as *Hockley in the Hole*, for three of the Ladies, for one
in *Vinegar Yard*, and for the rest of them somewhere about
Lewkner's Lane. Sure some of them are below, for I hear the Barr   25
Bell. As they come I will show them up. Coming, Coming.

SCENE IV

MACHEATH, MRS COAXER, DOLLY TRULL, MRS VIXEN,
BETTY DOXY, JENNY DIVER, MRS SLAMMEKIN, SUKY
TAWDRY, *and* MOLLY BRAZEN.

MACHEATH. Dear Mrs. *Coaxer*, you are welcome. You look
charmingly to-day. I hope you don't want the Repairs of Quality,
and lay on Paint.—*Dolly Trull*! kiss me, you Slut; are you as
amorous as ever, Hussy? You are always so taken up with stealing
Hearts, that you don't allow your self Time to steal any thing   5
else.—Ah *Dolly*, thou wilt ever be a Coquette!—Mrs. *Vixen*, I'm
yours, I always lov'd a Woman of Wit and Spirit; they make
charming Mistresses, but plaguy Wives.—*Betty Doxy*! Come
hither, Hussy. Do you drink as hard as ever? You had better
stick to good wholesome Beer; for in troth, *Betty*, Strong-Waters   10
will in time ruin your Constitution. You should leave those to
your Betters.—What! and my pretty *Jenny Diver* too! As prim and
demure as ever! There is not any Prude, though ever so high bred,
hath a more sanctify'd Look, with a more mischievous Heart.
Ah! thou art a dear artful Hypocrite.—Mrs. *Slammekin*! as care-   15
less and genteel as ever! all you fine Ladies, who know your own
Beauty, affect an Undress.—But see, here's *Suky Tawdry* come to
contradict what I was saying. Every thing she gets one way she
lays out upon her Back. Why, *Suky*, you must keep at least a dozen
Tally-men. *Molly Brazen*!   20

She kisses him.

That's well done. I love a free-hearted Wench. Thou hast a most
agreeable Assurance, Girl, and art as willing as a Turtle.—But
hark! I hear musick. The Harper is at the Door. *If Musick be the
Food of Love, play on.* E'er you seat your selves, Ladies, what think
you of a Dance? Come in.   25

Enter HARPER.

Play the *French* Tune, that Mrs. *Slammekin* was so fond of.

A Dance a la ronde *in the* French *Manner;
near the End of it this Song and Chorus.*

AIR XXII. Cotillon.

⟨MACHEATH.⟩ *Youth's the Season made for Joys,*
        Love is then our Duty,
    She alone who that employs,
        Well deserves her Beauty.   30
        Let's be gay,
        While we may,
        Beauty's a Flower, despis'd in decay.
⟨CHORUS.⟩ *Youth's the Season &c.*

⟨MACHEATH.⟩ *Let us drink and sport to-day,*   35
        Ours is not to-morrow.
    Love with Youth flies swift away,
        Age is nought but Sorrow.
        Dance and sing,
        Time's on the Wing,   40
        Life never knows the return of Spring.
CHORUS. *Let us drink &c.*

MACHEATH. Now, pray Ladies, take your Places. Here Fellow,

                      Pays the HARPER.

Bid the Drawer bring us more Wine.

                      Exit HARPER.

If any of the Ladies chuse Ginn, I hope they will be so free to call   45
for it.

JENNY DIVER. You look as if you meant me. Wine is strong
enough for me. Indeed, Sir, I never drink Strong-Waters, but
when I have the Cholic.

MACHEATH. Just the Excuse of the fine Ladies! Why, a Lady of   50
Quality is never without the Cholic. I hope, Mrs. *Coaxer*, you
have had good Success of late in your Visits among the Mercers.

MRS COAXER. We have so many Interlopers—Yet with Industry,
one may still have a little Picking. I carried a silver flower'd
Lutestring, and a Piece of black Padesoy to Mr. *Peachum*'s Lock   55
but last Week.

MRS VIXEN. There's *Molly Brazen* hath the Ogle of a Rattle-
Snake. She rivetted a Linnen-draper's Eye so fast upon her, that he
was nick'd of three Pieces of Cambric before he could look off.

MOLLY BRAZEN.   Oh dear Madam!—But sure nothing can come   60
up to your handling of Laces! And then you have such a sweet
deluding Tongue! To cheat a Man is nothing; but the Woman
must have fine Parts indeed who cheats a Woman!

MRS VIXEN.   Lace, Madam, lyes in a small Compass, and is of
easy Conveyance. But you are apt, Madam, to think too well of   65
your Friends.

MRS COAXER.   If any Woman hath more Art than another, to be
sure, 'tis *Jenny Diver*. Though her Fellow be never so agreeable, she
can pick his Pocket as cooly, as if Money were her only Pleasure.
Now that is a Command of the Passions uncommon in a Woman!   70

JENNY DIVER.   I never go to the Tavern with a Man, but in the
View of Business. I have other Hours, and other sort of Men for
my Pleasure. But had I your Address, Madam —

MACHEATH.   Have done with your Compliments, Ladies; and
drink about: You are not so fond of me, *Jenny*, as you use to be.   75

JENNY DIVER.   'Tis not convenient, Sir, to show my Fondness
among so many Rivals. 'Tis your own Choice, and not the warmth
of my Inclination that will determine you.

AIR XXIII.   All in a misty Morning, *&c.*

Before the Barn-door crowing,
The Cock by Hens attended,   80
His Eyes around him throwing,
Stands for a while suspended.
Then One he singles from the Crew,
And cheers the happy Hen;
With how do you do, and how do you do,   85
And how do you do again.

MACHEATH.   Ah *Jenny*! thou art a dear Slut.

DOLLY TRULL.   Pray, Madam, were you ever in keeping?

SUKY TAWDRY.   I hope, Madam, I ha'nt been so long upon the
Town, but I have met with some good Fortune as well as my   90
Neighbours.

DOLLY TRULL.   Pardon me, Madam, I meant no harm by the
Question; 'twas only in the way of Conversation.

SUKY TAWDRY.   Indeed, Madam, if I had not been a Fool, I might
have liv'd very handsomely with my last Friend. But upon his   95
missing five Guineas, he turn'd me off. Now I never suspected he
had counted them.

MRS SLAMMEKIN.   Who do you look upon, Madam, as your best
sort of Keepers?

DOLLY TRULL.   That, Madam, is thereafter as they be.   100

MRS SLAMMEKIN.   I, Madam, was once kept by a *Jew*; and bating
their Religion, to Women they are a good sort of People.

SUKY TAWDRY.   Now for my part, I own I like an old Fellow: for
we always make them pay for what they can't do.

MRS VIXEN.   A spruce Prentice, let me tell you, Ladies, is no ill   105
thing, they bleed freely. I have sent at least two or three dozen of
them in my time to the Plantations.

JENNY DIVER.   But to be sure, Sir, with so much good Fortune
as you have had upon the Road, you must be grown immensely
rich.   110

MACHEATH.   The Road, indeed, hath done me justice, but the
Gaming-Table hath been my ruin.

AIR XXIV.   When once I lay with another Man's Wife, *&c.*

JENNY DIVER.
    The Gamesters and Lawyers are Jugglers alike,
      If they meddle your All is in danger.
    Like Gypsies, if once they can finger a Souse,   115
    Your Pockets they pick, and they pilfer your House,
      And give your Estate to a Stranger.

A Man of Courage should never put any Thing to the Risque, but
his Life. These are the Tools of a Man of Honour. Cards and Dice
are only fit for cowardly Cheats, who prey upon their Friends.   120

                She takes up his Pistol. SUKY
             TAWDRY *takes up the other.*

SUKY TAWDRY.   This, Sir, is fitter for your Hand. Besides your
Loss of Money, 'tis a Loss to the Ladies. Gaming takes you off
from Women. How fond could I be of you! but before Company,
'tis ill bred.

MACHEATH.   Wanton Hussies!   125

JENNY DIVER.   I must and will have a Kiss to give my Wine a
zest.

       They take him about the Neck, and make Signs to
      PEACHUM *and Constables, who rush in upon him.*

SCENE V

To them, PEACHUM *and Constables.*

PEACHUM.   I seize you, Sir, as my Prisoner.

MACHEATH.   Was this well done, *Jenny*?—Women are Decoy
Ducks; who can trust them! Beasts, Jades, Jilts, Harpies, Furies,
Whores!

PEACHUM.   Your Case, Mr. *Macheath,* is not particular. The greatest   5
Heroes have been ruin'd by Women. But, to do them justice,
I must own they are a pretty sort of Creatures, if we could trust
them. You must now, Sir, take your leave of the Ladies, and if
they have a Mind to make you a Visit, they will be sure to find you
at home. The Gentleman, Ladies, lodges in *Newgate.* Constables,   10
wait upon the Captain to his Lodgings.

AIR XXV.   When first I laid Siege to my *Chloris,* &c.

MACHEATH.   *At the Tree I shall suffer with pleasure,*
              At the Tree I shall suffer with pleasure,
                 Let me go where I will,
                 In all kinds of Ill,   15
              I shall find no such Furies as these are.

PEACHUM.   Ladies, I'll take care the Reckoning shall be discharg'd.

                              Exit MACHEATH, *guarded with*
                                 PEACHUM *and Constables.*

SCENE VI

The Women remain.

MRS VIXEN.   Look ye, Mrs. *Jenny,* though Mr. *Peachum* may
have made a private Bargain with you and *Suky Tawdry* for
betraying the Captain, as we were all assisting, we ought all to
share alike.

MRS COAXER.   I think Mr. *Peachum,* after so long an acquaintance,   5
might have trusted me as well as *Jenny Diver.*

MRS SLAMMEKIN.   I am sure at least three Men of his hanging, and in a Year's time too, (if he did me justice) should be set down to my account.

DOLLY TRULL. Mrs. *Slammekin*, that is not fair. For you know　10
one of them was taken in Bed with me.

JENNY DIVER. As far as a Bowl of Punch or a Treat, I believe Mrs.
Suky will join with me.—As for any thing else, Ladies, you
cannot in conscience expect it.

MRS SLAMMEKIN. Dear Madam —　　　15

DOLLY TRULL. I would not for the World —

MRS SLAMMEKIN. 'Tis impossible for me —

DOLLY TRULL. As I hope to be sav'd, Madam —

MRS SLAMMEKIN. Nay, then I must stay here all Night —

DOLLY TRULL. Since you command me.　　　20

Exeunt with great Ceremony.

SCENE VII

Newgate.

LOCKIT, *Turnkeys*, MACHEATH, *Constables*.

LOCKIT. Noble Captain, you are welcome. You have not been a
Lodger of mine this Year and half. You know the custom,
Sir. Garnish, Captain, Garnish. Hand me down those Fetters
there.

MACHEATH. Those, Mr. *Lockit*, seem to be the heaviest of the　5
whole sett. With your leave, I should like the further pair better.

LOCKIT. Look ye, Captain, we know what is fittest for our
Prisoners. When a Gentleman uses me with Civility, I always do
the best I can to please him.—Hand them down I say.—We have
them of all Prices, from one Guinea to ten, and 'tis fitting every　10
Gentleman should please himself.

MACHEATH. I understand you, Sir.

Gives Money.

The Fees here are so many, and so exorbitant, that few Fortunes
can bear the Expence of getting off handsomly, or of dying like a
Gentleman.　　　15

LOCKIT. Those, I see, will fit the Captain better.—Take down the
further Pair. Do but examine them, Sir.—Never was better work.

—How genteely they are made!—They will sit as easy as a Glove, and the nicest Man in *England* might not be asham'd to wear them.

He puts on the Chains.

If I had the best Gentleman in the Land in my Custody I could not   20 equip him more handsomly. And so, Sir—I now leave you to your private Meditations.

SCENE VIII

MACHEATH.

AIR XXVI.   Courtiers, Courtiers think it no harm, *&c.*

Man may escape from Rope and Gun;
Nay, some have out-liv'd the Doctor's Pill;
Who takes a Woman must be undone,
*   That Basilisk is sure to kill.*
The Fly that sips Treacle is lost in the Sweets,   5
So he that tastes Woman, Woman, Woman,
*   He that tastes Woman, Ruin meets.*

To what a woful plight have I brought my self! Here must I (all day long, 'till I am hang'd) be confin'd to hear the Reproaches of a Wench who lays her Ruin at my Door.—I am in the Custody   10 of her Father, and to be sure if he knows of the matter, I shall have a fine time on't betwixt this and my Execution.—But I promis'd the Wench Marriage.—What signifies a Promise to a Woman? Does not Man in Marriage itself promise a hundred things that he never means to perform? Do all we can, Women will believe us; for they   15 look upon a Promise as an Excuse for following their own Inclinations.—But here comes *Lucy*, and I cannot get from her—Wou'd I were deaf!

SCENE IX

MACHEATH, LUCY.

LUCY.　You base Man you,—how can you look me in the Face after what hath past between us?—See here, perfidious Wretch, how I am forc'd to bear about the load of Infamy you have laid upon me —O *Macheath*! thou hast robb'd me of my Quiet—to see thee tortur'd would give me pleasure.　　　5

AIR XXVII.　A lovely Lass to a Friar came, *&c.*

> *Thus when a good Huswife sees a Rat*
> *In her Trap in the Morning taken,*
> *With pleasure her Heart goes pit a pat,*
> *In Revenge for her loss of Bacon.*
> 　　*Then she throws him*　　　10
> 　　　*To the Dog or Cat,*
> *To be worried, crush'd and shaken.*

MACHEATH.　Have you no Bowels, no Tenderness, my dear *Lucy*, to see a Husband in these Circumstances?

LUCY.　A Husband!　　　15

MACHEATH.　In ev'ry respect but the Form, and that, my Dear, may be said over us at any time.—Friends should not insist upon Ceremonies. From a Man of Honour, his Word is as good as his Bond.

LUCY.　'Tis the Pleasure of all you fine Men to insult the Women　20 you have ruin'd.

AIR XXVIII.　'Twas when the Sea was roaring, *&c.*

> *How cruel are the Traytors,*
> 　　*Who lye and swear in jest,*
> *To cheat unguarded Creatures*
> 　　*Of Virtue, Fame, and Rest!*　　　25
> *Whoever steals a Shilling,*
> 　　*Through Shame the Guilt conceals:*
> *In Love the perjur'd Villain*
> 　　*With Boasts the Theft reveals.*

MACHEATH.   The very first Opportunity, my Dear, (have but   30
Patience) you shall be my Wife in whatever manner you please.

LUCY.   Insinuating Monster! And so you think I know nothing of
the Affair of Miss *Polly Peachum.*—I could tear thy Eyes out!

MACHEATH.   Sure *Lucy*, you can't be such a Fool as to be jealous
of *Polly*!   35

LUCY.   Are you not married to her, you Brute, you?

MACHEATH.   Married! Very good. The Wench gives it out only
to vex thee, and to ruin me in thy good Opinion. 'Tis true, I go to
the House; I chat with the Girl, I kiss her, I say a thousand things
to her (as all Gentlemen do) that mean nothing, to divert my self;   40
and now the silly Jade hath set it about that I am married to her,
to let me know what she would be at. Indeed, my dear *Lucy*, these
violent Passions may be of ill consequence to a Woman in your
condition.

LUCY.   Come, come, Captain, for all your Assurance, you know   45
that Miss *Polly* hath put it out of your power to do me the Justice
you promis'd me.

MACHEATH.   A jealous Woman believes ev'ry thing her Passion
suggests. To convince you of my Sincerity, if we can find the
Ordinary, I shall have no Scruples of making you my Wife; and I   50
know the consequence of having two at a time.

LUCY.   That you are only to be hang'd, and so get rid of them both.

MACHEATH.   I am ready, my dear *Lucy*, to give you satisfaction—
if you think there is any in Marriage.—What can a Man of Honour
say more?   55

LUCY.   So then it seems, you are not married to Miss *Polly*.

MACHEATH.   You know, *Lucy*, the Girl is prodigiously conceited.
No Man can say a civil thing to her, but (like other fine Ladies) her
Vanity makes her think he's her own for ever and ever.

AIR XXIX.   The Sun had loos'd his weary Teams, *&c.*

> *The first time at the Looking-glass*   60
> *The Mother sets her Daughter,*
> *The Image strikes the smiling Lass*
> *With Self-love ever after.*
> *Each time she looks, she, fonder grown,*
> *Thinks ev'ry Charm grows stronger.*   65
> *But alas, vain Maid, all Eyes but your own*
> *Can see you are not younger.*

When Women consider their own Beauties, they are all alike
unreasonable in their demands; for they expect their Lovers should
like them as long as they like themselves.   70
LUCY.   Yonder is my Father—perhaps this way we may light upon
the Ordinary, who shall try if you will be as good as your Word.—
For I long to be made an honest Woman.

SCENE X

PEACHUM, LOCKIT *with an Account-Book.*

LOCKIT.   In this last Affair, Brother *Peachum*, we are agreed. You
have consented to go halves in *Macheath*.
PEACHUM.   We shall never fall out about an Execution.—But as
to that Article, pray how stands our last Year's account?
LOCKIT.   If you will run your Eye over it, you'll find 'tis fair and   5
clearly stated.
PEACHUM.   This long Arrear of the Government is very hard upon
us! Can it be expected that we should hang our Acquaintance for
nothing, when our Betters will hardly save theirs without being
paid for it. Unless the People in employment pay better, I promise   10
them for the future, I shall let other Rogues live besides their own.
LOCKIT.   Perhaps, Brother, they are afraid these matters may be
carried too far. We are treated too by them with Contempt, as if
our Profession were not reputable.
PEACHUM.   In one respect indeed, our Employment may be   15
reckon'd dishonest, because, like Great Statesmen, we encourage
those who betray their Friends.
LOCKIT.   Such Language, Brother, any where else, might turn to
your prejudice. Learn to be more guarded, I beg you.

AIR XXX.   How happy are we, &c.

When you censure the Age,   20
Be cautious and sage,
Lest the Courtiers offended should be:
If you mention Vice or Bribe,
'Tis so pat to all the Tribe;
Each crys—That was levell'd at me.   25

PEACHUM.   Here's poor *Ned Clincher*'s Name, I see. Sure, Brother *Lockit*, there was a little unfair proceeding in *Ned*'s case: for he told me in the Condemn'd Hold, that for Value receiv'd, you had promis'd him a Session or two longer without Molestation.

LOCKIT.   Mr. *Peachum*,—This is the first time my Honour was   30
ever call'd in Question.

PEACHUM.   Business is at an end—if once we act dishonourably.

LOCKIT.   Who accuses me?

PEACHUM.   You are warm, Brother.

LOCKIT.   He that attacks my Honour, attacks my Livelyhood.—   35
And this Usage—Sir—is not to be born.

PEACHUM.   Since you provoke me to speak—I must tell you too, that Mrs. *Coaxer* charges you with defrauding her of her Informa-tion-Money, for the apprehending of curl-pated *Hugh*. Indeed, indeed, Brother, we must punctually pay our Spies, or we shall   40
have no Information.

LOCKIT.   Is this Language to me, Sirrah—who have sav'd you from the Gallows, Sirrah!

Collaring each other.

PEACHUM.   If I am hang'd, it shall be for ridding the World of an arrant Rascal.   45

LOCKIT.   This Hand shall do the office of the Halter you deserve, and throttle you—you Dog! —

PEACHUM.   Brother, Brother,—We are both in the Wrong—We shall be both Losers in the Dispute—for you know we have it in our Power to hang each other. You should not be so passionate.   50

LOCKIT.   Nor you so provoking.

PEACHUM.   'Tis our mutual Interest; 'tis for the Interest of the World we should agree. If I said any thing, Brother, to the Pre-judice of your Character, I ask pardon.

LOCKIT.   Brother *Peachum*—I can forgive as well as resent.—   55
Give me your Hand. Suspicion does not become a Friend.

PEACHUM.   I only meant to give you occasion to justifie yourself: But I must now step home, for I expect the Gentleman about this Snuff-box, that *Filch* nimm'd two Nights ago in the Park. I appointed him at this hour.   60

SCENE XI

LOCKIT, LUCY.

LOCKIT. Whence come you, Hussy?

LUCY. My Tears might answer that Question.

LOCKIT. You have then been whimpering and fondling, like a Spaniel, over the Fellow that hath abus'd you.

LUCY. One can't help Love; one can't cure it. 'Tis not in my   5
Power to obey you, and hate him.

LOCKIT. Learn to bear your Husband's Death like a reasonable Woman. 'Tis not the fashion, now-a-days, so much as to affect Sorrow upon these Occasions. No Woman would ever marry, if she had not the Chance of Mortality for a Release. Act like a   10
Woman of Spirit, Hussy, and thank your Father for what he is doing.

AIR XXXI. Of a noble Race was *Shenkin.*

LUCY. *Is then his Fate decreed, Sir?*
        Such a Man can I think of quitting?
        When first we met, so moves me yet,   15
        O see how my Heart is splitting!

LOCKIT. Look ye, *Lucy*—There is no saving him.—So, I think, you must ev'n do like other Widows—Buy your self Weeds, and be cheerful.

AIR XXXII.

You'll think e'er many Days ensue   20
    This Sentence not severe;
I hang your Husband, Child, 'tis true,
    But with him hang your Care.
    Twang dang dillo dee.

Like a good Wife, go moan over your dying Husband. That,   25
Child, is your Duty—Consider, Girl, you can't have the Man and the Money too—so make yourself as easy as you can, by getting all you can from him.

SCENE XII

LUCY, MACHEATH.

LUCY. Though the Ordinary was out of the way to-day, I hope,
my Dear, you will, upon the first opportunity, quiet my Scruples—
Oh Sir!—my Father's hard Heart is not to be soften'd, and I am in
the utmost Despair.

MACHEATH.   But if I could raise a small Sum—Would not twenty   5
Guineas, think you, move him?—Of all the Arguments in the way
of Business, the Perquisite is the most prevailing.—Your Father's
Perquisites for the Escape of Prisoners must amount to a considerable Sum in the Year. Money well tim'd, and properly apply'd, will
do any thing.   10

AIR XXXIII.   *London* Ladies.

If you at an Office solicit your Due,
    And would not have Matters neglected;
You must quicken the Clerk with the Perquisite too,
    To do what his Duty directed.
Or would you the Frowns of a Lady prevent,   15
    She too has this palpable Failing,
The Perquisite softens her into Consent;
    That Reason with all is prevailing.

LUCY. What Love or Money can do shall be done: for all my
Comfort depends upon your Safety.   20

SCENE XIII

LUCY, MACHEATH, POLLY.

POLLY.   Where is my dear Husband?—Was a Rope ever intended
for this Neck!—O let me throw my Arms about it, and throttle
thee with Love!—Why dost thou turn away from me?—'Tis thy
Polly—'Tis thy Wife.

MACHEATH.   Was ever such an unfortunate Rascal as I am!   5

LUCY. Was there ever such another Villain!

POLLY. O *Macheath!* was it for this we parted? Taken! Imprison'd! Try'd! Hang'd!—cruel Reflection! I'll stay with thee 'till Death— no Force shall tear thy dear Wife from thee now.—What means my Love?—Not one kind Word! not one kind Look! think what 10 thy *Polly* suffers to see thee in this Condition.

AIR XXXIV. All in the Downs, &c.

Thus when the Swallow, seeking Prey,
 Within the Sash is closely pent,
His Consort, with bemoaning Lay,
 Without sits pining for th' Event. 15
Her chatt'ring Lovers all around her skim;
She heeds them not (poor Bird!) her Soul's with him.

MACHEATH. [*Aside.*] I must disown her. ⟨*Aloud.*⟩ The Wench is distracted.

LUCY. Am I then bilk'd of my Virtue? Can I have no Reparation? 20 Sure Men were born to lye, and Women to believe them! O Villain! Villain!

POLLY. Am I not thy Wife?—Thy Neglect of me, thy Aversion to me too severely proves it.—Look on me.—Tell me, am I not thy Wife? 25

LUCY. Perfidious Wretch!

POLLY. Barbarous Husband!

LUCY. Hadst thou been hang'd five Months ago, I had been happy.

POLLY. And I too—If you had been kind to me 'till Death, it would not have vex'd me—And that's no very unreasonable 30 Request, (though from a Wife) to a Man who hath not above seven or eight Days to live.

LUCY. Art thou then married to another? Hast thou two Wives, Monster?

MACHEATH. If Women's Tongues can cease for an Answer—hear 35 me.

LUCY. I won't.—Flesh and Blood can't bear my Usage.

POLLY. Shall I not claim my own? Justice bids me speak.

AIR XXXV.   Have you heard of a frolicksome Ditty, &c.

MACHEATH.   *How happy could I be with either,*
Were t'other dear Charmer away!   40
But while you thus teaʒe me together,
To neither a Word will I say;
But tol de rol, &c.

POLLY.   Sure, my Dear, there ought to be some Preference shown
to a Wife! At least she may claim the Appearance of it. He must be   45
distracted with his Misfortunes, or he could not use me thus!

LUCY.   O Villain, Villain! thou hast deceiv'd me—I could even
inform against thee with Pleasure. Not a Prude wishes more
heartily to have Facts against her intimate Acquaintance, than I
now wish to have Facts against thee. I would have her Satisfaction,   50
and they should all out.

AIR XXXVI.   *Irish* Trot.

POLLY.   *I'm bubbled.*
LUCY.   ———————— *I'm bubbled.*
POLLY.   *Oh how I am troubled!*
LUCY.   *Bambouʒled, and bit!*   55
POLLY.   ———————————— *My Distresses are doubled.*
LUCY.   *When you come to the Tree, should the Hangman refuse,*
These Fingers, with Pleasure, could fasten the Noose.
POLLY.   *I'm bubbled,* &c.

MACHEATH.   Be pacified, my dear *Lucy*—This is all a Fetch of   60
Polly's, to make me desperate with you in case I get off. If I am
hang'd, she would fain have the Credit of being thought my
Widow—Really, *Polly*, this is no time for a Dispute of this sort;
for whenever you are talking of Marriage, I am thinking of Hanging.   65

POLLY.   And hast thou the Heart to persist in disowning me?

MACHEATH.   And hast thou the Heart to persist in persuading me
that I am married? Why, *Polly*, dost thou seek to aggravate my
Misfortunes?

LUCY.   Really, Miss *Peachum*, you but expose yourself. Besides,   70
'tis barbarous in you to worry a Gentleman in his Circumstances.

AIR XXXVII.

POLLY.   *Cease your Funning;*
               Force or Cunning
        Never shall my Heart trapan.
                  All these Sallies   75
                  Are but Malice
        To seduce my constant Man.
           'Tis most certain,
           By their flirting
        Women oft' have Envy shown;   80
           Pleas'd, to ruin
           Others wooing;
        Never happy in their own!

Decency, Madam, methinks might teach you to behave yourself
with some Reserve with the Husband, while his Wife is present.   85
MACHEATH.   But seriously, *Polly*, this is carrying the Joke a little
too far.
LUCY.   If you are determin'd, Madam, to raise a Disturbance in the
Prison, I shall be oblig'd to send for the Turnkey to show you the
Door. I am sorry, Madam, you force me to be so ill-bred.   90
POLLY.   Give me leave to tell you, Madam; These forward Airs
don't become you in the least, Madam. And my Duty, Madam,
obliges me to stay with my Husband, Madam.

AIR XXXVIII.   Good-morrow, Gossip *Joan*.

LUCY.   *Why how now, Madam* Flirt?
        If you thus must chatter;   95
    And are for flinging Dirt,
        Let's try who best can spatter;
                Madam Flirt!
POLLY.   *Why how now, saucy Jade;*
        Sure the Wench is Tipsy!   100
    How can you see me made   [*To him.*
        The Scoff of such a Gipsy?
                Saucy Jade!   [*To her.*

SCENE XIV

LUCY, MACHEATH, POLLY, PEACHUM.

PEACHUM.   Where's my Wench? Ah Hussy! Hussy!— Come you
home, you Slut; and when your Fellow is hang'd, hang yourself,
to make your Family some amends.

POLLY.   Dear, dear Father, do not tear me from him—I must
speak; I have more to say to him—Oh! twist thy Fetters about me,   5
that he may not haul me from thee!

PEACHUM.   Sure all Women are alike! If ever they commit the
Folly, they are sure to commit another by exposing themselves—
Away—Not a Word more—You are my Prisoner now, Hussy.

AIR XXXIX.   *Irish* Howl.

POLLY.   *No Power on Earth can e'er divide,*   10
The Knot that Sacred Love hath ty'd.
When Parents draw against our Mind,
The True-love's Knot they faster bind.
    Oh, oh ray, oh Amborah—oh, oh, &c.

[*Holding* MACHEATH, PEACHUM *pulling her.*

SCENE XV

LUCY, MACHEATH.

MACHEATH.   I am naturally compassionate, Wife; so that I could
not use the Wench as she deserv'd; which made you at first suspect
there was something in what she said.

LUCY.   Indeed, my Dear, I was strangely puzzled.

MACHEATH.   If that had been the Case, her Father would never   5
have brought me into this Circumstance—No, *Lucy*,—I had
rather dye than be false to thee.

LUCY.   How happy am I, if you say this from your Heart! For I
love thee so, that I could sooner bear to see thee hang'd than in the
Arms of another.   10

MACHEATH.   But couldst thou bear to see me hang'd?

LUCY.   O *Macheath*, I can never live to see that Day.

MACHEATH. You see, *Lucy*; in the Account of Love you are in my
debt, and you must now be convinc'd, that I rather chuse to die
than be another's.—Make me, if possible, love thee more, and let 15
me owe my Life to thee—If you refuse to assist me, *Peachum* and
your Father will immediately put me beyond all means of Escape.

LUCY. My Father, I know, hath been drinking hard with the
Prisoners: and I fancy he is now taking his Nap in his own Room—
If I can procure the Keys, shall I go off with thee, my Dear? 20

MACHEATH. If we are together, 'twill be impossible to lye conceal'd. As soon as the Search begins to be a little cool, I will send to
thee—'Till then my Heart is thy Prisoner.

LUCY. Come then, my dear Husband—owe thy Life to me—and
though you love me not—be grateful—But that *Polly* runs in my 25
Head strangely.

MACHEATH. A Moment of time may make us unhappy for-ever.

AIR XL. The Lass of *Patie*'s Mill, &c.

LUCY. *I like the Fox shall grieve,*
 Whose Mate hath left her side,
Whom Hounds, from Morn to Eve, 30
 Chase o'er the Country wide.
Where can my Lover hide?
 Where cheat the weary Pack?
If Love be not his Guide,
 He never will come back! 35

II.XV.33 *we ary*] FE, SEI; *wary* SE2–9, TE. *This difficult crux is discussed in
the Textual Notes.*

ACT III

SCENE I

SCENE *Newgate.*

LOCKIT, LUCY.

LOCKIT. To be sure, Wench, you must have been aiding and abetting to help him to this Escape.

LUCY. Sir, here hath been *Peachum* and his Daughter *Polly*, and to be sure they know the Ways of *Newgate* as well as if they had been born and bred in the Place all their Lives. Why must all your Suspicion light upon me? 5

LOCKIT. *Lucy*, *Lucy*, I will have none of these shuffling Answers.

LUCY. Well then—If I know any Thing of him I wish I may be burnt!

LOCKIT. Keep your Temper, *Lucy*, or I shall pronounce you guilty. 10

LUCY. Keep yours, Sir,—I do wish I may be burnt. I do—And what can I say more to convince you?

LOCKIT. Did he tip handsomely?—How much did he come down with? Come Hussy, don't cheat your Father; and I shall not be angry with you—Perhaps, you have made a better Bargain with him than I could have done—How much, my good Girl? 15

LUCY. You know, Sir, I am fond of him, and would have given Money to have kept him with me.

LOCKIT. Ah *Lucy*! thy Education might have put thee more upon thy Guard; for a Girl in the Bar of an Ale-house is always besieg'd. 20

LUCY. Dear Sir, mention not my Education—for 'twas to that I owe my Ruin.

AIR XLI.   If Love's a sweet Passion, *&c.*

When young at the Bar you first taught me to score,
And bid me be free of my Lips, and no more; 25
I was kiss'd by the Parson, the Squire, and the Sot.
When the Guest was departed, the Kiss was forgot.
But his Kiss was so sweet, and so closely he prest,
That I languish'd and pin'd 'till I granted the rest.

If you can forgive me, Sir, I will make a fair Confession, for to   30
be sure he hath been a most barbarous Villain to me.

LOCKIT.   And so you have let him escape, Hussy—Have you?

LUCY.   When a Woman loves; a kind Look, a tender Word can
persuade her to any thing—And I could ask no other Bribe.

LOCKIT.   Thou wilt always be a vulgar Slut, *Lucy*.—If you would   35
not be look'd upon as a Fool, you should never do any thing but
upon the Foot of Interest. Those that act otherwise are their own
Bubbles.

LUCY.   But Love, Sir, is a Misfortune that may happen to the most
discreet Woman, and in Love we are all Fools alike.—Notwith-   40
standing all he swore, I am now fully convinc'd that *Polly Peachum*
is actually his Wife.—Did I let him escape, (Fool that I was!) to
go to her?—*Polly* will wheedle herself into his Money, and then
Peachum will hang him, and cheat us both.

LOCKIT.   So I am to be ruin'd, because, forsooth, you must be in   45
Love!—a very pretty Excuse!

LUCY.   I could murder that impudent happy Strumpet:—I gave
him his Life, and that Creature enjoys the Sweets of it.—Ungrate-
ful *Macheath*!

AIR XLII.   *South-Sea* Ballad.

My Love is all Madness and Folly,   50
     Alone I lye,
  Toss, tumble, and cry,
What a happy Creature is Polly!
Was e'er such a Wretch as I!
With Rage I redden like Scarlet,   55
That my dear inconstant Varlet,
     Stark blind to my Charms,
     Is lost in the Arms
Of that Jilt, that inveigling Harlot!
     Stark blind to my Charms,   60
     Is lost in the Arms
Of that Jilt, that inveigling Harlot!
This, this my Resentment alarms.

LOCKIT.   And so, after all this Mischief, I must stay here to be
entertain'd with your catterwauling, Mistress Puss!— Out of my   65

Sight, wanton Strumpet! you shall fast and mortify yourself into Reason, with now and then a little handsome Discipline to bring you to your Senses.—Go.

SCENE II

LOCKIT.

Peachum then intends to outwit me in this Affair; but I'll be even with him.—The Dog is leaky in his Liquor, so I'll ply him that way, get the Secret from him, and turn this Affair to my own Advantage.—Lions, Wolves, and Vulturs don't live together in Herds, Droves or Flocks.—Of all Animals of Prey, Man is the only 5 sociable one. Every one of us preys upon his Neighbour, and yet we herd together.—*Peachum* is my Companion, my Friend— According to the Custom of the World, indeed, he may quote thousands of Precedents for cheating me—And shall not I make use of the Privilege of Friendship to make him a Return? 10

AIR XLIII. *Packington*'s Pound.

> *Thus Gamesters united in Friendship are found,*
> *Though they know that their Industry all is a Cheat;*
> *They flock to their Prey at the Dice-Box's Sound,*
> *And join to promote one another's Deceit.*
> *   But if by mishap* 15
> *   They fail of a Chap,*
> *To keep in their Hands, they each other entrap.*
> *Like Pikes, lank with Hunger, who miss of their Ends,*
> *They bite their Companions, and prey on their Friends.*

Now, *Peachum*, you and I, like honest Tradesmen, are to have a 20 fair Tryal which of us two can over-reach the other.—*Lucy.* —

Enter LUCY.

Are there any of *Peachum*'s People now in the House?
LUCY. *Filch*, Sir, is drinking a Quartern of Strong-Waters in the next Room with Black *Moll*.
LOCKIT. Bid him come to me. 25

SCENE III

LOCKIT, FILCH.

LOCKIT.   Why, Boy, thou lookest as if thou wert half starv'd; like a shotten Herring.

FILCH.   One had need have the Constitution of a Horse to go thorough the Business.—Since the favourite Child-getter was disabled by a Mis-hap, I have pick'd up a little Money by helping   5
the Ladies to a Pregnancy against their being call'd down to Sentence.—But if a Man cannot get an honest Livelyhood any easier way, I am sure, 'tis what I can't undertake for another Session.

LOCKIT.   Truly, if that great Man should tip off, 'twould be an irreparable Loss. The Vigor and Prowess of a Knight-Errant never   10
sav'd half the Ladies in Distress that he hath done.—But, Boy, can'st thou tell me where thy Master is to be found?

FILCH.   At his *Lock, Sir, at the *Crooked Billet.*

LOCKIT.   Very well.—I have nothing more with you.

Exit FILCH.

I'll go to him there, for I have many important Affairs to settle   15
with him; and in the way of those Transactions, I'll artfully get into his Secret.—So that *Macheath* shall not remain a Day longer out of my Clutches.

SCENE IV

A Gaming-House.

MACHEATH *in a fine tarnish'd Coat,* BEN BUDGE, MATT OF THE MINT.

MACHEATH.   I am sorry, Gentlemen, the Road was so barren of Money. When my Friends are in Difficulties, I am always glad that my Fortune can be serviceable to them.

Gives them Money.

---

* A Cant Word, signifying, a Warehouse where stolen Goods are deposited.

You see, Gentlemen, I am not a meer Court Friend, who professes
every thing and will do nothing.   5

AIR XLIV.   Lillibullero.

The Modes of the Court so common are grown,
*   That a true Friend can hardly be met;*
Friendship for Interest is but a Loan,
*   Which they let out for what they can get.*
*   'Tis true, you find*   10
*   Some Friends so kind,*
Who will give you good Counsel themselves to defend.
*   In sorrowful Ditty,*
*   They promise, they pity,*
But shift you for Money, from Friend to Friend.   15

But we, Gentlemen, have still Honour enough to break through
the Corruptions of the World.—And while I can serve you, you
may command me.

BEN BUDGE.   It grieves my Heart that so generous a Man should
be involv'd in such Difficulties, as oblige him to live with such ill   20
Company, and herd with Gamesters.

MATT OF THE MINT.   See the Partiality of Mankind!—One Man
may steal a Horse, better than another look over a Hedge—Of all
Mechanics, of all servile Handycrafts-men, a Gamester is the
vilest. But yet, as many of the Quality are of the Profession, he is   25
admitted amongst the politest Company. I wonder we are not
more respected.

MACHEATH.   There will be deep Play to-night at *Marybone*, and
consequently Money may be pick'd up upon the Road. Meet me
there, and I'll give you the Hint who is worth Setting.   30

MATT OF THE MINT.   The Fellow with a brown Coat with a
narrow Gold Binding, I am told, is never without Money.

MACHEATH.   What do you mean, *Matt?*—Sure you will not think
of meddling with him!—He's a good honest kind of a Fellow, and
one of us.   35

BEN BUDGE.   To be sure, Sir, we will put our selves under your
Direction.

MACHEATH.   Have an Eye upon the Money-Lenders.—A *Rouleau*,
or two, would prove a pretty sort of an Expedition. I hate Extor-
tion.   40

MATT OF THE MINT. Those *Rouleaus* are very pretty Things.—
I hate your Bank Bills.—There is such a Hazard in putting them off.
MACHEATH. There is a certain Man of Distinction, who in his
Time hath nick'd me out of a great deal of the Ready. He is in my
Cash, *Ben*;—I'll point him out to you this Evening, and you shall   45
draw upon him for the Debt.—The Company are met; I hear the
Dice-box in the other Room. So, Gentlemen, your Servant. You'll
meet me at *Marybone*.

SCENE V

Peachum'*s* *Lock*.

A Table with Wine, Brandy, Pipes and Tobacco.

PEACHUM, LOCKIT.

LOCKIT. The Coronation Account, Brother *Peachum*, is of so
intricate a Nature, that I believe it will never be settled.
PEACHUM. It consists indeed of a great Variety of Articles.— It
was worth to our People, in Fees of different Kinds, above ten
Instalments.—This is part of the Account, Brother, that lies open   5
before us.
LOCKIT. A Lady's Tail of rich Brocade—that, I see, is dispos'd of.
PEACHUM. To Mrs. *Diana Trapes*, the Tally-woman, and she will
make a good Hand on't in Shoes and Slippers, to trick out young
Ladies, upon their going into Keeping. —   10
LOCKIT. But I don't see any Article of the Jewels.
PEACHUM. Those are so well known, that they must be sent
abroad—You'll find them enter'd under the Article of Exportation.
—As for the Snuff-Boxes, Watches, Swords, *&c.*—I thought it best
to enter them under their several Heads.   15
LOCKIT. Seven and twenty Women's Pockets compleat; with the
several things therein contain'd; all Seal'd, Number'd, and enter'd.
PEACHUM. But, Brother, it is impossible for us now to enter upon
this Affair.—We should have the whole Day before us.—Besides,
the Account of the last Half Year's Plate is in a Book by it self,   20
which lies at the other Office.
LOCKIT. Bring us then more Liquor.—To-day shall be for
Pleasure—To-morrow   for   Business.—Ah   Brother,   those

Daughters of ours are two slippery Hussies—Keep a watchful Eye
upon *Polly*, and *Macheath* in a Day or two shall be our own again.   25

AIR XLV.   Down in the North Country, &c.

> *What Gudgeons are we Men!*
> *Ev'ry Woman's easy Prey.*
> *Though we have felt the Hook, agen*
> *We bite and they betray.*

> *The Bird that hath been trapt,*   30
> *When he hears his calling Mate,*
> *To her he flies, again he's clapt*
> *Within the wiry Grate.*

PEACHUM.   But what signifies catching the Bird, if your Daughter
Lucy will set open the Door of the Cage?   35
LOCKIT.   If Men were answerable for the Follies and Frailties of
their Wives and Daughters, no Friends could keep a good Correspondence together for two Days.—This is unkind of you, Brother;
for among good Friends, what they say or do goes for nothing.

Enter a SERVANT.

SERVANT.   Sir, here's Mrs. *Diana Trapes* wants to speak with you.   40
PEACHUM.   Shall we admit her, Brother *Lockit*?
LOCKIT.   By all means—She's a good Customer, and a fine-spoken
Woman—And a Woman who drinks and talks so freely, will
enliven the Conversation.
PEACHUM.   Desire her to walk in.   45

Exit SERVANT.

SCENE VI

PEACHUM, LOCKIT, MRS TRAPES.

PEACHUM.   Dear Mrs. *Dye*, your Servant—One may know by your
Kiss, that your Ginn is excellent.
MRS TRAPES.   I was always very curious in my Liquors.
LOCKIT.   There is no perfum'd Breath like it—I have been long
acquainted with the Flavour of those Lips—Han't I, Mrs. *Dye*?   5

MRS TRAPES. Fill it up.—I take as large Draughts of Liquor, as
I did of Love.—I hate a Flincher in either.

AIR XLVI.   A Shepherd kept Sheep, &c.

In the Days of my Youth I could bill like a Dove, fa, la, la, &c.
Like a Sparrow at all times was ready for Love, fa, la, la, &c.
The Life of all Mortals in Kissing should pass,   10
Lip to Lip while we're young—then the Lip to the Glass, fa, &c.

But now, Mr. *Peachum*, to our Business.—If you have Blacks of
any kind, brought in of late; Mantoes—Velvet Scarfs—Petticoats
—Let it be what it will—I am your Chap—for all my Ladies are
very fond of Mourning.   15
PEACHUM.   Why, look ye, Mrs. *Dye*—you deal so hard with us,
that we can afford to give the Gentlemen, who venture their Lives
for the Goods, little or nothing.
MRS TRAPES.   The hard Times oblige me to go very near in my
Dealing.—To be sure, of late Years I have been a great Sufferer   20
by the Parliament.—Three thousand Pounds would hardly make
me amends.—The Act for destroying the Mint, was a severe Cut
upon our Business—'Till then, if a Customer stept out of the way—
we knew where to have her—No doubt you know Mrs. *Coaxer*—
there's a Wench now ('till to-day) with a good Suit of Cloaths of   25
mine upon her Back, and I could never set Eyes upon her for three
Months together.—Since the Act too against Imprisonment for
small Sums, my Loss there too hath been very considerable, and it
must be so, when a Lady can borrow a handsome Petticoat, or a
clean Gown, and I not have the least Hank upon her! And, o' my   30
Conscience, now-a-days most Ladies take a Delight in cheating,
when they can do it with Safety.
PEACHUM.   Madam, you had a handsome Gold Watch of us
t'other Day for seven Guineas.—Considering we must have our
Profit—To a Gentleman upon the Road, a Gold Watch will be   35
scarce worth the taking.
MRS TRAPES.   Consider, Mr. *Peachum*, that Watch was remark-
able, and not of very safe Sale.—If you have any black Velvet
Scarfs—they are a handsome Winter-wear; and take with most
Gentlemen who deal with my Customers.—'Tis I that put the   40
Ladies upon a good Foot. 'Tis not Youth or Beauty that fixes their

Price. The Gentlemen always pay according to their Dress, from half a Crown to two Guineas; and yet those Hussies make nothing of bilking of me.—Then too, allowing for Accidents.—I have eleven fine Customers now down under the Surgeon's Hands,— 45 what with Fees and other Expences, there are great Goings-out, and no Comings-in, and not a Farthing to pay for at least a Month's cloathing.—We run great Risques—great Risques indeed.

PEACHUM. As I remember, you said something just now of Mrs. *Coaxer*. 50

MRS TRAPES. Yes, Sir.—To be sure I stript her of a Suit of my own Cloaths about two hours ago; and have left her as she should be, in her Shift, with a Lover of hers at my House. She call'd him up Stairs, as he was going to *Marybone* in a Hackney Coach.— And I hope, for her own sake and mine, she will perswade the Captain 55 to redeem her, for the Captain is very generous to the Ladies.

LOCKIT. What Captain?

MRS TRAPES. He thought I did not know him—An intimate Acquaintance of yours, Mr. *Peachum*—Only Captain *Macheath*— as fine as a Lord. 60

PEACHUM. To-morrow, dear Mrs. *Dye*, you shall set your own Price upon any of the Goods you like—We have at least half a dozen Velvet Scarfs, and all at your service. Will you give me leave to make you a Present of this Suit of Night-cloaths for your own wearing?—But are you sure it is Captain *Macheath*? 65

MRS TRAPES. Though he thinks I have forgot him; no Body knows him better. I have taken a great deal of the Captain's Money in my Time at second-hand, for he always lov'd to have his Ladies well drest.

PEACHUM. Mr. *Lockit* and I have a little business with the Captain; 70 —You understand me—and we will satisfye you for Mrs. *Coaxer*'s Debt.

LOCKIT. Depend upon it—we will deal like Men of Honour.

MRS TRAPES. I don't enquire after your Affairs—so whatever happens, I wash my Hands on't.—It hath always been my Maxim, 75 that one Friend should assist another—But if you please—I'll take one of the Scarfs home with me, 'Tis always good to have something in Hand.

SCENE VII

Newgate.

LUCY.

Jealousy, Rage, Love and Fear are at once tearing me to pieces. How I am weather-beaten and shatter'd with distresses!

AIR XLVII.   One Evening, having lost my Way, *&c.*

> *I'm like a Skiff on the Ocean tost,*
> *Now high, now low, with each Billow born,*
> *With her Rudder broke, and her Anchor lost,*   5
> *Deserted and all forlorn.*
> *While thus I lye rolling and tossing all Night,*
> *That* Polly *lyes sporting on Seas of Delight!*
> *Revenge, Revenge, Revenge,*
> *Shall appease my restless Sprite.*   10

I have the Rats-bane ready.—I run no Risque; for I can lay her Death upon the Ginn, and so many dye of that naturally that I shall never be call'd in Question.—But say, I were to be hang'd— I never could be hang'd for any thing that would give me greater Comfort, than the poysoning that Slut.   15

Enter FILCH.

FILCH.   Madam, here's our Miss *Polly* come to wait upon you.
LUCY.   Show her in.

SCENE VIII

LUCY, POLLY.

LUCY.   Dear Madam, your Servant.—I hope you will pardon my Passion, when I was so happy to see you last.—I was so over-run with the Spleen, that I was perfectly out of my self. And really when one hath the Spleen, every thing is to be excus'd by a Friend.

AIR XLVIII. Now *Roger*, I'll tell thee, because thou'rt my Son.

> *When a Wife's in her Pout,*   5
> *(As she's sometimes, no doubt;)*
>   *The good Husband as meek as a Lamb,*
>   *Her Vapours to still,*
>   *First grants her her Will,*
>   *And the quieting Draught is a Dram.*   10
> *Poor Man! And the quieting Draught is a Dram.*

—I wish all our Quarrels might have so comfortable a Reconciliation.

POLLY.   I have no Excuse for my own Behaviour, Madam, but my Misfortunes.—And really, Madam, I suffer too upon your Account.   15

LUCY.   But, Miss *Polly*—in the way of Friendship, will you give me leave to propose a Glass of Cordial to you?

POLLY.   Strong-Waters are apt to give me the Head-ache—I hope, Madam, you will excuse me.

LUCY.   Not the greatest Lady in the Land could have better in her   20
Closet, for her own private drinking.—You seem mighty low in Spirits, my Dear.

POLLY.   I am sorry, Madam, my Health will not allow me to accept of your Offer.—I should not have left you in the rude Manner I did when we met last, Madam, had not my Papa haul'd me away   25
so unexpectedly—I was indeed somewhat provok'd, and perhaps might use some Expressions that were disrespectful.—But really, Madam, the Captain treated me with so much Contempt and Cruelty, that I deserv'd your Pity, rather than your Resentment.

LUCY.   But since his Escape, no doubt all Matters are made up again.   30
—Ah *Polly*! *Polly*! 'tis I am the unhappy Wife; and he loves you as if you were only his Mistress.

POLLY.   Sure, Madam, you cannot think me so happy as to be the Object of your Jealousy.—A Man is always afraid of a Woman who loves him too well—so that I must expect to be neglected and   35
avoided.

LUCY.   Then our Cases, my dear *Polly*, are exactly alike. Both of us indeed have been too fond.

AIR XLIX.   O *Bessy Bell.*

POLLY.   *A Curse attends that Woman's Love,*
              Who always would be pleasing.   40
LUCY.   *The Pertness of the billing Dove,*
              Like tickling, is but teazing.
POLLY.   *What then in Love can Woman do?*
LUCY.   *If we grow fond they shun us.*
POLLY.   *And when we fly them, they pursue.*   45
LUCY.   *But leave us when they've won us.*

Love is so very whimsical in both Sexes, that it is impossible to be lasting.—But my Heart is particular, and contradicts my own Observation.

POLLY.   But really, Mistress *Lucy*, by his last Behaviour, I think I   50
ought to envy you.—When I was forc'd from him, he did not shew the least Tenderness.—But perhaps, he hath a Heart not capable of it.

AIR L.   Would Fate to me *Belinda* give —

Among the Men, Coquets we find,
Who Court by turns all Woman-kind;   55
And we grant all their Hearts desir'd,
When they are flatter'd, and admir'd.

The Coquets of both Sexes are Self-lovers, and that is a Love no other whatever can dispossess. I fear, my dear *Lucy*, our Husband is one of those.   60

LUCY.   Away with these melancholy Reflections,—indeed, my dear *Polly*, we are both of us a Cup too low.—Let me prevail upon you, to accept of my Offer.

AIR LI.   Come, sweet Lass, *&c.*

Come, sweet Lass,
Let's banish Sorrow   65
'Till To-morrow;
Come, sweet Lass,
Let's take a chirping Glass.
Wine can clear
The Vapours of Despair;   70
And make us light as Air;
Then drink, and banish Care.

I can't bear, Child, to see you in such low Spirits.— And I must
persuade you to what I know will do you good.—[*Aside.*] I shall
now soon be even with the hypocritical Strumpet.   75

SCENE IX

POLLY.

All this wheedling of *Lucy* cannot be for nothing.—At this time
too! when I know she hates me!—The Dissembling of a Woman is
always the Fore-runner of Mischief.—By pouring Strong-Waters
down my Throat, she thinks to pump some Secrets out of me.—
I'll be upon my Guard, and won't taste a Drop of her Liquor, I'm   5
resolv'd.

SCENE X

LUCY, *with Strong-Waters.* POLLY.

LUCY.   Come, Miss *Polly.*

POLLY.   Indeed, Child, you have given yourself trouble to no
purpose.—You must, my Dear, excuse me.

LUCY.   Really, Miss *Polly*, you are so squeamishly affected about
taking a Cup of Strong-Waters as a Lady before Company. I vow,   5
Polly, I shall take it monstrously ill if you refuse me.—Brandy and
Men (though Women love them never so well) are always taken by
us with some Reluctance—unless 'tis in private.

POLLY.   I protest, Madam, it goes against me.—What do I see!
Macheath again in Custody!—Now every glimm'ring of Happi-   10
ness is lost.

Drops the Glass of Liquor on the Ground.

LUCY.   [*Aside.*]   Since things are thus, I'm glad the Wench hath
escap'd: for by this Event, 'tis plain, she was not happy enough to
deserve to be poison'd.

SCENE XI

LOCKIT, MACHEATH, PEACHUM, LUCY, POLLY.

LOCKIT.   Set your Heart to rest, Captain.—You have neither the Chance of Love or Money for another Escape,—for you are order'd to be call'd down upon your Tryal immediately.

PEACHUM.   Away, Hussies!—This is not a time for a Man to be hamper'd with his Wives.—You see, the Gentleman is in Chains   5
already.

LUCY.   O Husband, Husband, my Heart long'd to see thee; but to see thee thus distracts me!

POLLY.   Will not my dear Husband look upon his *Polly*? Why hadst thou not flown to me for Protection? with me thou hadst   10
been safe.

AIR LII.   The last time I went o'er the Moor.

POLLY.   *Hither, dear Husband, turn your Eyes.*
LUCY.   *Bestow one Glance to cheer me.*
POLLY.   *Think with that Look, thy* Polly *dyes.*
LUCY.   *O shun me not—but hear me.*   15
POLLY.   *'Tis* Polly *sues.*
LUCY.   ———————— *'Tis* Lucy *speaks.*
POLLY.   *Is thus true Love requited?*
LUCY.   *My Heart is bursting.*
POLLY.   ——————— *Mine too breaks.*   20
LUCY.   *Must I*
POLLY.   ——————— *Must I be slighted?*

MACHEATH.   What would you have me say, Ladies?—You see, this Affair will soon be at an end, without my disobliging either of you.   25

PEACHUM.   But the settling this Point, Captain, might prevent a Law-suit between your two Widows.

E

AIR LIII.   *Tom Tinker*'s my true Love.

MACHEATH.   *Which way shall I turn me?—How can I decide?*
Wives, the Day of our Death, are as fond as a Bride.
One Wife is too much for most Husbands to hear,   30
But two at a time there's no Mortal can bear.
This way, and that way, and which way I will,
What would comfort the one, t'other Wife would take ill.

POLLY.   But if his own Misfortunes have made him insensible to
mine—A Father sure will be more compassionate.—Dear, dear Sir,   35
sink the material Evidence, and bring him off at his Tryal—*Polly*
upon her Knees begs it of you.

AIR LIV.   I am a poor Shepherd undone.

When my Hero in Court appears,
    And stands arraign'd for his Life;
Then think of poor Polly's *Tears;*   40
    For Ah! Poor Polly's *his Wife.*
Like the Sailor he holds up his Hand,
    Distrest on the dashing Wave.
To die a dry Death at Land,
    Is as bad as a watry Grave.   45
And alas, poor Polly!
Alack, and well-a-day!
Before I was in Love,
    Oh! every Month was May.

LUCY.   If *Peachum*'s Heart is harden'd; sure you, Sir, will have more   50
Compassion on a Daughter.—I know the Evidence is in your
Power.—How then can you be a Tyrant to me?

                                        Kneeling.

AIR LV.   *Ianthe* the lovely, *&c.*

When he holds up his Hand arraign'd for his Life,
O think of your Daughter, and think I'm his Wife!
What are Cannons, or Bombs, or clashing of Swords?   55
For Death is more certain by Witnesses Words.
Then nail up their Lips; that dread Thunder allay;
And each Month of my Life will hereafter be May.

LOCKIT. *Macheath*'s time is come, *Lucy*.—We know our own
Affairs, therefore let us have no more Whimpering or Whining. 60

AIR LVI. A Cobler there was, *&c.*

Our selves, like the Great, to secure a Retreat,
When Matters require it, must give up our Gang:
    And good reason why,
    Or, instead of the Fry,
    Ev'n Peachum *and I,* 65
Like poor petty Rascals, might hang, hang;
Like poor petty Rascals, might hang.

PEACHUM. Set your Heart at rest, *Polly*.—Your Husband is to
dye to-day.—Therefore, if you are not already provided, 'tis high
time to look about for another. There's Comfort for you, you Slut. 70
LOCKIT. We are ready, Sir, to conduct you to the *Old-Baily*.

AIR LVII. Bonny *Dundee.*

MACHEATH. *The Charge is prepar'd; The Lawyers are met,*
    The Judges all rang'd (a terrible Show!)
    I go, undismay'd.—For Death is a Debt,
    A Debt on demand.—So, take what I owe. 75
    Then farewell, my Love—Dear Charmers, adieu.
    Contented I die—'Tis the better for you.
    Here ends all Dispute the rest of our Lives.
    For this way at once I please all my Wives.

Now, Gentlemen, I am ready to attend you. 80

SCENE XII

LUCY, POLLY, FILCH.

POLLY. Follow them, *Filch*, to the Court. And when the Tryal is
over, bring me a particular Account of his Behaviour, and of every
thing that happen'd.—You'll find me here with Miss *Lucy*.

Exit FILCH.

But why is all this Musick?

LUCY. The Prisoners, whose Tryals are put off till next Session, 5
are diverting themselves.

POLLY. Sure there is nothing so charming as Musick! I'm fond of it
to distraction!—But alas!—now, all Mirth seems an Insult upon my
Affliction.—Let us retire, my dear *Lucy*, and indulge our Sorrows.
—The noisy Crew, you see, are coming upon us. 10

Exeunt.

A Dance of Prisoners in Chains, &c.

SCENE XIII

The Condemn'd Hold.

MACHEATH, *in a melancholy Posture.*

AIR LVIII. Happy Groves.

O cruel, cruel, cruel Case!
Must I suffer this Disgrace?

AIR LIX. Of all the Girls that are so smart.

Of all the Friends in time of Grief,
When threatning Death looks grimmer,
Not one so sure can bring Relief, 5
As this best Friend, a Brimmer. [*Drinks.*

AIR LX. *Britons* strike home.

Since I must swing,—I scorn, I scorn to wince or whine.
[*Rises.*

AIR LXI. Chevy Chase.

But now again my Spirits sink;
I'll raise them high with Wine. [*Drinks a Glass of Wine.*

AIR LXII. To old Sir *Simon* the King.

But Valour the stronger grows, 10
The stronger Liquor we're drinking.
And how can we feel our Woes,
When we've lost the Trouble of Thinking? [*Drinks.*

AIR LXIII.   Joy to great *Caesar.*

If thus—A Man can die
Much bolder with Brandy.   [*Pours out a Bumper of Brandy.*   15

AIR LXIV.   There was an Old Woman.

So I drink off this Bumper.—And now I can stand the Test.
And my Comrades shall see, that I die as brave as the Best.

[*Drinks.*

AIR LXV.   Did you ever hear of a gallant Sailor.

But can I leave my pretty Hussies,
Without one Tear, or tender Sigh?

AIR LXVI.   Why are mine Eyes still flowing.

Their Eyes, their Lips, their Busses   20
Recall my Love.—Ah must I die!

AIR LXVII.   Green Sleeves.

Since Laws were made for ev'ry Degree,
  To curb Vice in others, as well as me,
  I wonder we han't better Company,
    Upon Tyburn *Tree!*   25
    But Gold from Law can take out the Sting;
    And if rich Men like us were to swing,
    'Twou'd thin the Land, such Numbers to string
      Upon Tyburn *Tree!*

⟨*Enter* JAILOR.⟩

JAILOR.   Some Friends of yours, Captain, desire to be admitted.—   30
I leave you together.

SCENE XIV

MACHEATH, BEN BUDGE, MATT OF THE MINT.

MACHEATH.   For my having broke Prison, you see, Gentlemen, I
am order'd immediate Execution.—The Sheriffs Officers, I believe,
are now at the Door.—That *Jemmy Twitcher* should peach me, I
own surpriz'd me!—'Tis a plain Proof that the World is all alike,

and that even our Gang can no more trust one another than other   5
People. Therefore, I beg you, Gentlemen, look well to yourselves,
for in all probability you may live some Months longer.

MATT OF THE MINT. We are heartily sorry, Captain, for your
Misfortune.—But 'tis what we must all come to.

MACHEATH. *Peachum* and *Lockit*, you know, are infamous   10
Scoundrels. Their Lives are as much in your Power, as yours are in
theirs.—Remember your dying Friend!—'Tis my last Request.
—Bring those Villains to the Gallows before you, and I am
satisfied.

MATT OF THE MINT. We'll do't.   15

⟨*Enter* JAILOR.⟩

JAILOR. Miss *Polly* and Miss *Lucy* intreat a Word with you.
MACHEATH. Gentlemen, adieu.

SCENE XV

LUCY, MACHEATH, POLLY.

MACHEATH. My dear *Lucy*—My dear *Polly*—Whatsoever hath
past between us is now at an end.—If you are fond of marrying
again, the best Advice I can give you, is to Ship yourselves off for
the *West-Indies*, where you'll have a fair chance of getting a
Husband a-piece; or by good Luck, two or three, as you like best.   5

POLLY. How can I support this Sight!
LUCY. There is nothing moves one so much as a great Man in
Distress.

AIR LXVIII. All you that must take a Leap, &c.

LUCY.	*Would I might be hang'd!*
POLLY.	————————————*And I would so too!* 10
LUCY.	*To be hang'd with you.*
POLLY.	———————————— *My Dear, with you.*
MACHEATH.	*O Leave me to Thought! I fear! I doubt!*
	I tremble! I droop!—See, my Courage is out.

[*Turns up the empty Bottle.*

POLLY.   *No token of Love?*   15
MACHEATH.   ———————— *See, my Courage is out.*

                         [*Turns up the empty Pot.*

LUCY.   *No token of Love?*
POLLY.   ———————— *Adieu.*
LUCY.   ———————————— *Farewell.*
MACHEATH.   *But hark! I hear the Toll of the Bell.*   20
CHORUS.   *Tol de rol lol,* &c.

⟨*Enter* JAILOR.⟩

JAILOR. Four Women more, Captain, with a Child a-peice! See,
here they come.

Enter Women and Children.

MACHEATH. What—four Wives more!—This is too much.—
Here—tell the Sheriffs Officers I am ready.   25

                         Exit MACHEATH *guarded.*

                         SCENE XVI

               To them, Enter PLAYER *and* BEGGAR.

PLAYER. But, honest Friend, I hope you don't intend that *Macheath* shall be really executed.
BEGGAR. Most certainly, Sir.—To make the Piece perfect, I was
for doing strict poetical Justice.—*Macheath* is to be hang'd; and for
the other Personages of the Drama, the Audience must have   5
suppos'd they were all either hang'd or transported.
PLAYER. Why then, Friend, this is a down-right deep Tragedy.
The Catastrophe is manifestly wrong, for an Opera must end
happily.
BEGGAR. Your Objection, Sir, is very just; and is easily remov'd.   10
For you must allow, that in this kind of Drama, 'tis no matter how
absurdly things are brought about.—So—you Rabble there—run
and cry a Reprieve—let the Prisoner be brought back to his Wives
in Triumph.
PLAYER. All this we must do, to comply with the Taste of the   15
Town.

BEGGAR.   Through the whole Piece you may observe such a simili-
tude of Manners in high and low Life, that it is difficult to determine
whether (in the fashionable Vices) the fine Gentlemen imitate the
Gentlemen of the Road, or the Gentlemen of the Road the fine   20
Gentlemen.—Had the Play remain'd, as I at first intended, it would
have carried a most excellent Moral. 'Twould have shown that the
lower Sort of People have their Vices in a degree as well as the
Rich: And that they are punish'd for them.

SCENE XVII

To them, MACHEATH *with Rabble,* &c.

MACHEATH.   So, it seems, I am not left to my Choice, but must
have a Wife at last.—Look ye, my Dears, we will have no Con-
troversie now. Let us give this Day to Mirth, and I am sure she who
thinks herself my Wife will testifie her Joy by a Dance.
ALL.   Come, a Dance—a Dance.   5
MACHEATH.   Ladies, I hope you will give me leave to present a
Partner to each of you. And (if I may without Offence) for this
time, I take *Polly* for mine.— ⟨*To* POLLY.⟩   And for Life, you
Slut,—for we were really marry'd.— ⟨*Aloud.*⟩   As for the
rest.— [*To* POLLY.]   But at present keep your own Secret.   10

A DANCE.

AIR LXIX.   Lumps of Pudding, *&c.*

Thus I stand like the Turk, *with his Doxies around;*
From all Sides their Glances his Passion confound;
For black, brown, and fair, his Inconstancy burns,
And the different Beauties subdue him by turns:
Each calls forth her Charms, to provoke his Desires: 15
Though willing to all; with but one he retires.
But think of this Maxim, and put off your Sorrow,
The Wretch of To-day, may be happy To-morrow.
CHORUS.   *But think of this Maxim,* &c.

FINIS

TEXTUAL NOTES

COMMENTARY

BIBLIOGRAPHY

F

TEXTUAL NOTES

A TABLE OF THE SONGS

AIR 27   *Huswife*] SE9,TE; *Huswise* SEI–8.
AIR 28   *Traytors.*] ~ , SEI–8; *Traitors,*
   SE9; *traytors,* TE.
AIR 32   *ensue.*] ~ ᴧ SE, TE.
AIR 38   *Flirt?*] ~ . SE, TE.
AIR 53   *decide?*] ~ . SE; *om.* TE.
AIR 57   *The Lawyers*] *the* ~ SE, TE.

DRAMATIS PERSONAE

MATT] Mat FE, SE, TE.

THE NAMES OF THE LILLIPUTIANS

Ben . . . *Woodward*] SE6–9; ~ . . .
   Wodward SE5.

I. II

29 S.H.   gray-ey'd] SE; grey-ey'd FE.

I. III

7   Snuff-boxes] *The hyphen appears in
   all copies of* SE *examined, but only in a
   few copies of* FE, *and even then it
   prints imperfectly. There is no trace of
   it in* FEI–3, *but it does print faintly in
   most copies of* FE4–5. *It would seem
   that a damaged or defective piece of
   type was set for* FEI *and that it failed
   to print until the later impressions of*
   FE. *It must have been replaced during
   the reimposition of the type for* SE.
   *Elsewhere in the text the words are
   hyphenated.*

I. IV

72   Livelihood] SE; livelihood FE.

I. VI

44 a   Glass   of   a   most   delicious
   Cordial] SE; a most delicious Glass
   of a Cordial FE.

I. VII

9–16   *Alternate lines of Air VI are
   indented in* SE, *but not in* FE.

I. VIII

1   have] SE; *om.* FE.

I. IX

23   *picking,*] SE; ~ ; FE.
24   *Chicken;*] ~ ; SE; ~ , FE.

I. X

23   Hope] SE; hope FE.
59   Love] SE; love FE.

I. XIII

30 S.H.   XVI] FE5, SE; VI FEI–4.
43   S.P. *is repeated in* FE, SE, TE.

II. I

D.P.   HENRY PADINGTON] *Elsewhere in* FE, SE *and* TE *this character is called* Harry *not* Henry, *but since Gay himself was almost certainly responsible for this anomaly, I have preserved it.*
31   Injury] SE; injury FE.

II. II

50   *Fire their Fire*] SE; *fire ~ fire* FE.
51 S.D.   *Chorus.*] Chorus. TE; Chorus, FE, SE.

II. III

D.P.   MACHEATH.] *Macheath, Drawer.* FE, SE; *MACHEATH, DRAWER.* TE. *Macheath is alone at the opening of this scene. The Drawer does not enter until later.* D.P. *in* FE, SE, TE *is therefore misleading.*
1   S.P. *is repeated in* FE, SE, TE.
25   Lewkner's Lane] TE; *Lewkner's Lane* FE, SE. *The reading of* FE, *retained in* SE, *is anomalous and patently compositorial rather than authorial.*

II. IV

41   *In* FE *and* SE *this long line is aligned with lines 35, 37 and 42, but since it*
rhymes with the two short lines preceding it, it should almost certainly be aligned with them, as is the corresponding line (33) in the first stanza. The compositor of* TE *effected a compromise by aligning both these lines with the second and fourth lines of each stanza.*
44 S.D.   *Exit*] *Ex.* FE, SE, TE.
118–9   A Man . . . Life.] SE; *om.* FE.
120 S.D.   SUKY] *om.* FE, SE, TE.

II. V

17 S.D.   *Exit*] *Ex.* FE, SE, TE.

II. VII

D.P.   MACHEATH] *MACHEATH* TE; Mackheath FE, SE.
18   sit] *Although long* s *followed by* i *looks very similar to* fi, *there can be no doubt that all eighteenth century editions listed in the Bibliography except for one read* sit. *The Seventh Edition (London, 1745) reads* set *(this is not an emendation, but an error caused by the substitution of* e *for* i, *one of the easiest mistakes to make in type-setting). However all the twentieth century editions examined except for Edward J. Dent's edition of the music ('45' in the Bibliography), which gives only the words of the songs and consequently does not include this speech, and the photographic reprint of* TE *('46' in the Bibliography) read* fit. *Twentieth century editors have either silently emended the word or, what is almost certainly the case, misread long* s *as* f *because* fit *is the word one would now automatically use in this context. Verbal expectation seems to have blinded editors to the actual letter and word on the page. Nevertheless the fact that* sit *was not replaced by* fit *in any of the eighteenth century editions means that* sit *seemed perfectly natural to Gay's contemporaries. If* sit *had*

originally been a compositorial error, or even a manuscript error reproduced by the compositor of FE, it would not have persisted in the way it did. The errors and irregularities of FE did not survive for long in subsequent eighteenth century editions. It is therefore certain that Gay wrote and intended sit. The appearance of fit earlier in the same speech and of fittest and fitting in Lockit's previous speech confirms this, because Gay would not have wanted to repeat the word again.

II. IX

5 S.H.   AIR _Λ] TE; ~ . FE, SE.

10–1 *These two lines are considerably less indented in* SE *than in* FE.

18   Honour] SE; honour FE.

20   Pleasure] SE; pleasure FE.

27   *Shame*] SE; shame FE.

30   Opportunity] SE; opportunity FE.

31   Patience] SE; patience FE.

50   Scruples] SE; scruples FE.

II. X

19 S.H.   AIR _Λ] SE; ~ . FE.

II. XII

10 S.H.   *London*] SE; London FE.

II. XIII

51 S.H   *Irish*] Irish FE, SE, TE.

84   S.P. *is repeated in* FE, SE, TE.

II. XIV

9 S.H.   *Irish*] SE; Irish FE.

II. XV

2   suspect] SE; susspect FE.

27 S.H.   AIR _Λ] SE; ~ . FE.

33   weary] FE, SE1; *wary* SE2–9, TE. *This textual crux has never been adequately discussed. Most editions after* TE *give* 'wary', *but a few give* 'weary', *including G. Hamilton Macleod's edition (London, 1905). Most modern editors print* 'wary' *without being aware of the problem or without making any attempt to defend their adoption of this reading. In fact it is probably impossible to decide with absolute certainty which reading Gay intended. Both make sense although both can be criticised, and the bibliographical evidence is inconclusive. After running* 'from Morn to Eve', *the hounds would certainly be* 'weary' *as would the fox, but it could be argued that the fox, even a weary fox, should not have such a hard time escaping from* 'the weary Pack'. *At first sight* 'wary' *is an odd word to use to describe the hounds, being more applicable to the fox, but as the fox has to* 'cheat' *the hounds in order to escape,* 'wary' *is not inappropriate in this context. On the grounds of good sense, there is virtually nothing to choose between the two readings. The real difficulty comes in deciding whether* 'wary' *is an authorial emendation. If* 'wary' *had appeared in* SE1, *it would certainly have been an authorial correction, but there is nothing to suggest that* SE2 *carries more authority than* SE1. *Apart from this change and the failure of a damaged semi-colon in Air XXXVII in* SE1 *to print in* SE2, *the texts of* SE1 *and* SE2 *are identical. Corrections that could have been made to* SE1, *and that were made in* SE3, *were not made in* SE2. *The alteration is therefore very puzzling. If* 'weary' *was a compositorial error, there are two possibilities: (1) the printers were instructed to make the change to* 'wary' *when they were correcting and reimposing the type of* FE *for* SE1, *but failed to do so until*

SE2; (2) the error was not noticed until after the publication of SE1, although if this were the case it is difficult to understand why obvious errors in SE1 were not spotted and corrected in SE2. If 'weary' was not a compositorial error, there are also two possibilities: (1) the printers made the change to 'wary' without authority, either deliberately or accidentally; (2) Gay originally wrote 'weary' but subsequently decided that 'wary' would be preferable. Exactly what happened remains a matter of speculation. In the circumstances I have printed the original reading in the text and recorded the emendation at the foot of the page.

III. I

49 S.H.   *South-Sea*] SE; South-Sea FE.

III. III

10   Knight-Errant] SE; ∼ ∧ ∼ FE.
14 S.D.   *Exit*] *Ex.* FE, SE, TE.

III. V

26   S.P. *is repeated in* FE, SE, TE.

III. VIII

38 S.H.   *Bessy Bell*] TE; Bessy Bell FE, SE. *All other names and comparable words in the song-headings are italicised in* SE *except for* Irish *in Air* XXXVI.
47   S.P. *is repeated in* FE, SE, TE.
50   Behaviour,] SE; ∼ ; FE.

III. IX

IX] SE; X FE.
1   S.P. *is repeated in* FE, SE, TE.

III. XI

7   Heart] SE; heart FE.
40   Polly's] FE5, SE; Polly's FE1–4.
41   Polly's] FE5, SE; Polly's FE1–4.
45   *bad*] FE5, SE; *had* FE1–4.
60 S.H.–67   AIR . . . *hang.*] FE5, SE; *om.* FE1–4. *In* FE5 *the song is not numbered. The full-stop consequently follows* AIR, *not* LVI *as in* SE.

III. XII

3 S.D.   *Exit*] *Ex.* FE, SE, TE.

III. XIII.

0 S.D.   *The Condemn'd Hold*] TE; The Condemn'd Hold FE, SE. *In* FE *and* SE *all other scene locations are set substantially in italics. The use of roman type on this occasion was probably an error, although it may have been chosen deliberately to contrast with the predominantly italic setting of this Scene.*

III. XIV

D.P.   MATT] Mat FE, SE; *MAT* TE.

III. XV

22   a-peice] *This could be but is not necessarily a compositor's error. Though becoming rare,* peice *was still a variant spelling of* piece *in the eighteenth century, not a misspelling. Even though* a-piece *appears earlier in this scene (5) and* piece *is found elsewhere in the text, Gay may have written* a-peice *on this occasion. His spelling is by no means consistent, variant forms of other words appearing in the text. The fact that the compositors of* SE1 *(the re-set part) and* TE *retained* a-peice *suggests that it did not strike them as a compositorial error.*

COMMENTARY

DRAMATIS PERSONAE

The names of most of the characters are descriptive. Some, such as FILCH, MRS COAXER, MRS VIXEN and MOLLY BRAZEN, are still self-explanatory. Others require clarification.

PEACHUM] i.e. 'Peach 'em'. An appropriate name for a thief-taker, a man who 'peaches' criminals or brings them to justice by informing against them.

LOCKIT] i.e. 'Lock it'. An appropriate name for the chief jailor of Newgate Prison.

MACHEATH] i.e. 'Son of the heath'. An appropriate name for a highwayman, because the heaths around London, such as Hounslow Heath, were the usual scenes of highway robbery.

JEMMY TWITCHER] A 'twitcher' was a pickpocket.

ROBIN OF BAGSHOT] Bagshot Heath in Surrey was notorious for its highwaymen. Gay refers to the Heath in *An Epistle to the Right Honourable the Earl of Burlington* (21–2):

> Prepar'd for war, now *Bagshot-Heath* we cross,
> Where broken gamesters oft' repair their loss.

(See Commentary on I. III. 26–7 for a discussion of the significance of this name.)

NIMMING NED] To 'nim' was to steal.

HARRY PADINGTON] A 'pad' was a highwayman. Harry is a 'pad' from Paddington, the parish in which the gallows at Tyburn stood. An execution day was known as 'Paddington Fair Day', and 'to dance the Paddington frisk' was to be hanged.

MATT OF THE MINT] The Mint was an infamous district in Southwark that had been a virtual stronghold of debtors and criminals. (See Commentary on III. VI. 22.)

BEN BUDGE] A 'budge' was a thief, especially a burglar who stole cloaks and other clothes.

DIANA TRAPES] A 'trapes' was a slattern.

DOLLY TRULL] A 'trull' was a prostitute.

BETTY DOXY] A 'doxy' was a prostitute.

JENNY DIVER] A 'diver' was a pickpocket.

MRS SLAMMEKIN] A 'slammekin' was a slattern.

INTRODUCTION

By means of the dialogue between the Beggar and the Player, Gay virtually announces that one of his aims is to burlesque Italian opera. The Beggar solemnly claims that his work is a conventional opera, but it is obvious from his second speech that what he is about to present is a mock-opera. The Introduction therefore functions in a similar way to the ironic prefaces to two earlier plays, *The Mohocks* and *The What D'Ye Call It*, in which Gay establishes his burlesque intention by implication rather than by explicit statement.

3 make one at] take part in, join in.

3 St. *Giles's*] The parish of St Giles-in-the-Fields, near Holborn, housed many of London's beggars, whores and criminals.

4 Catches] musical rounds, popular songs in which the voices enter

successively singing the same words and melody.

14 *James Chanter* and *Moll Lay*] As their surnames indicate, these are type-figures, not real ballad singers. The linking of ballad singers with the disreputable inhabitants of St Giles-in-the-Fields is not fortuitous. Ballad singers were often considered to be the associates of criminals, as Gay points out in *Trivia* (III, 77–82):

Let not the ballad-singer's shrilling strain
Amid the swarm thy list'ning ear detain:
Guard well thy pocket; for these *Syrens* stand
To aid the labours of the diving hand;
Confed'rate in the cheat, they draw the throng,
And cambrick handkerchiefs reward the song.

15–7 the Similes . . . the *Flower*] 'The *Swallow*' appears in Air XXXIV, 'the *Moth*' in Air IV, 'the *Bee*' and 'the *Flower*' in Airs VI and XV, and 'the *Ship*' in Airs X and XLVII. It is unlikely that Gay is parodying any specific arias in these and similar songs, but he is burlesquing the use of such hackneyed similes in Italian opera by placing them in the mouths of low-life characters and setting them to well-known tunes.

17–8 a Prison Scene . . . charmingly pathetick] Few contemporary Italian operas lack a prison scene intended to be extremely pathetic and deeply moving. (See Bertrand H. Bronson's essay listed in the Bibliography for a full discussion of this point.) *The Beggar's Opera*, on the other hand, contains far more than one prison scene because much of the play is set in Newgate Prison. The 'Scene' that the Beggar refers to is probably the

part of the play set in the condemned cell (III. XIII–XV), although other scenes in Newgate involving Macheath, Polly and Lucy, such as II. XIII–XIV and III. XI, burlesque the sentimental prison scenes of opera.

18–20 As to the Parts . . . take Offence] An allusion to the bitter rivalry between Faustina Bordoni and Francesca Cuzzoni, the two leading ladies of Italian opera in London. Cuzzoni, who received a salary of £2000, was well established as a prima donna when Faustina was brought to London in the spring of 1726 at a salary of £2500. Their controversies over operatic roles and their personal enmity were never far from public attention during the period between Faustina's arrival in England and the first production of *The Beggar's Opera*. On one occasion, during a performance of Buononcini's *Astyanax* in 1727, the two prima donnas even came to blows on stage. This incident prompted an anonymous author to write the very amusing 'Small Farce', *The Contre Temps; or, Rival Queans* (1727), which ridicules the two sopranos as well as other notable figures associated with Italian opera in London, such as Handel and Heidegger. In *Alessandro*, the opera he wrote for Faustina's London début in May 1726, Handel tried to achieve 'a nice Impartiality' (nice: exact and careful) by creating two equally important female roles, Rossane and Lisaura, for the two singers, but his plan misfired. Instead of co-operating for the sake of the opera, Cuzzoni and Faustina competed with each other for public acclaim. Although there is no parody of *Alessandro* in *The Beggar's Opera*, Gay may have had Handel's opera particularly in mind when writing his play. The main action of *Alessandro*, concerning the love of both Rossane and Lisaura for Alessandro, resembles *The Beggar's Opera* in some respects, although similar situations are not rare in opera. In a general way the triangle of Polly, Lucy and Macheath does travesty the relationships between Rossane, Lisaura and Alessandro, but the burlesque is equally applicable to other operas. What is certain is that the struggle between Polly and Lucy over Macheath alludes satirically to the rivalry between Cuzzoni and Faustina. It is exceedingly ironic that in 1736 there was an acrimonious controversy between the two most famous actresses of the day, Kitty Clive and Susannah Cibber, over the part of Polly.

22 no Recitative] The use of recitative in Italian opera caused considerable bewilderment and amusement among English audiences at first, especially among hostile critics, as Addison's remarks in *The Spectator* No. 29 (3 April 1711) indicate: 'There is nothing that has more startled our *English* Audience, than the *Italian Recitativo* at its first Entrance upon the Stage. People were wonderfully surprized to hear Generals singing the Word of Command, and Ladies delivering Messages in Musick. Our Country-men could not forbear laughing when they heard a Lover chanting out a Billet-doux, and even the Superscription of a Letter set to a Tune. The Famous Blunder in an old Play of *Enter a King and two Fidlers Solus*, was now no longer an Absurdity, when it was impossible for a Hero in a Desart, or a Princess in her Closet, to speak any thing unaccompanied with Musical Instruments' (*The Spectator*, ed. D. F. Bond (Oxford, 1965), vol. I, pp. 119–20). In his 'opera' Gay uses dialogue, not

recitative, but Macheath's sung monologue in the death cell near the end of the play can be regarded as a mock-recitative. (See Commentary on III. XIII.)

23 neither Prologue nor Epilogue] Italian operas, unlike orthodox plays, were not provided with prologues and epilogues. Although dramatists constantly complained about the convention, virtually every eighteenth century tragedy and comedy is preceded by a prologue and followed by an epilogue. Frequently these were not written by the playwright but by a friend or another writer or an actor. Prologues, usually serious in tone, were normally spoken by actors, whereas epilogues, usually comic in spirit, were normally spoken by actresses.

29 the Overture] The Overture was written by the musical director of the Theatre Royal in Lincoln's Inn Fields, Johann Christoph Pepusch, who also arranged the music for the songs. Scored for oboes and strings, the Overture is in the French style and is contrapuntal in texture. It makes use of 'One evening having lost my way', which is also the tune of Air XLVII. The inclusion of an instrumental Overture in *The Beggar's Opera* emphasises its satirical parallel to Italian opera, but it is uncertain whether the Overture was part of Gay's original conception or a last-minute addition to the play. Some evidence suggests that Gay initially intended the Airs to be sung unaccompanied and that he had no plans for instrumental music. William Cooke states: 'To this Opera there was no music originally intended to accompany the songs, till Rich, the Manager, suggested it on the second last rehearsal. The junto of wits, who regularly attended, one and all,

objected to it; and it was given up till the Duchess of Queensbury (Gay's staunch patroness) accidentally hearing of it, attended herself the next rehearsal, when it was tried, and universally approved of' (*Memoirs of Charles Macklin, Comedian* (London, 1804), p. 60). If Cooke is correct, it means that the musical accompaniment for the songs was not even tried until the final rehearsal and that Pepusch arranged the music and probably provided the Overture as well between the last but one rehearsal and the first performance. On the face of it this seems very unlikely, especially as the actors would have had little chance to rehearse with the instrumentalists, but it is not impossible that the orchestral music was added at the very last moment. Dr Pepusch, a German from Berlin who had come to London in 1700 at the age of 33, had worked with Rich at Lincoln's Inn Fields for many years and could produce music for the theatre at great speed and under considerable pressure. The presence of the Player's words, 'Play away the Overture', in the First Edition, which was published very soon after the first performance, suggests that Gay wrote them before the final rehearsals, but the words could have been inserted into the manuscript presented to the publishers. The absence of the Overture from the First Edition and from the first issue of the Second Edition might give the impression that it was written shortly before the first performance, but other explanations are possible. The actual decision to provide an Overture must have been taken by Rich and Pepusch after the play had been accepted for production at Lincoln's Inn Fields, but Gay

may well have hoped all along that an Overture would be composed for *The Beggar's Opera* to enhance his burlesque of Italian opera.

I. I

7–8   *And the Statesman . . . as mine*] In his *Memoirs of the Life and Writings of Alexander Pope, Esq.* (London, 1745; vol. II, p. 115), William Ayre claims that Pope was responsible for the final wording of these two lines. According to Ayre, Gay wrote:

> And there's many arrive to be Great,
> By a Trade not more honest than mine.

Henry Angelo restates this claim in his *Reminiscences* (London, 1828; vol. I, p. 25).

I. II

4   plead her Belly] A woman convicted of a capital offence could not be executed while she was pregnant. If a pregnant woman was sentenced to death, she could 'plead her belly', this being the proper legal expression.

9   took] apprehended and brought to justice (by informing against).

12   forty Pounds] The reward for information resulting in the conviction of a man for a criminal offence. There was no reward in the case of a woman, as Peachum himself points out later in this scene. The reason for this discrimination between the sexes was simply that male criminals were far more numerous and presented a much greater threat to law and order than female criminals.

13   Transportation] The transportation of convicted criminals to the North American and West Indian colonies and plantations could be for life, but

was usually for seven or fourteen years. Later in the play Ben Budge talks about his 'Return from Transportation' (II. I. 2).

14 Lock] place where stolen goods were received and stored. (See Gay's own note at the foot of page 95.)

14 to-year] this year.

16 Customer] person with whom one has business dealings (not necessarily a purchaser, as in modern usage).

17 take her off] bring her to trial and execution (by informing against).

27–8 the Surgeons are more beholden to Women] In addition to being unpleasant, the treatment for venereal disease was long and costly. Peachum implies that the medical profession derived a great deal of financial benefit from venereal disease and were very much indebted to women suffering from it, particularly prostitutes, for transmitting it to men who could pay for a cure.

38 Newgate] London's main criminal prison was situated at the Old Bailey end of Newgate Street very close to the criminal court. Jonathan Wild, on whom Peachum is modelled, had lived near the prison and the court at 68 Old Bailey.

I. III

8 Handkerchiefs] The handkerchiefs of the well-to-do were made of lace or of expensive fabrics such as linen and silk, and were certainly worth stealing.

9 Tye-Perriwigs] wigs with the hair gathered at the back and tied with a ribbon.

9 Broad Cloth] fine black cloth used mainly for men's clothes.

11 prettier] finer.

15 petty-larceny Rascal] Petty larceny, a non-capital offence, was the theft of goods valued at less than a shilling.

Grand larceny, a capital offence, was the theft of property worth a shilling or more.

20 listed] enlisted.

25 to make others stand] 'stand' is used with the same meaning as in the highwayman's traditional cry, 'Stand and deliver'.

25 Cart] An open cart was used for taking condemned prisoners from Newgate to the gallows at Tyburn, where it functioned as a scaffold drop. 'Cart' is therefore a metonym of 'Execution' in this instance.

26–7 Robin of Bagshot . . . Bob Booty] Robin's aliases are satirical jibes at Walpole. 'Gorgon' and 'Carbuncle' are straightforward insults. 'Bluff Bob' suggests Walpole's alleged lack of refinement and of good manners and also his outspokenness, but there is a further suggestion that he bluffed his way through political life. 'Bob' itself carries criminal connotations because it was the slang term for a shoplifter's assistant. 'Bob Booty' implies the accusation often made against Walpole that he was a robber of the public, as does 'Robin of Bagshot'. Fielding also uses the homonymic resemblance between 'Robin' and 'robbing' to ridicule Walpole in his satirical ballad opera, The Grub-Street Opera (1731), in which Walpole appears as a cheating butler called Robin. Contemporary audiences, who were familiar with the wordplay on 'Robert' and 'robber' by anti-Government writers, immediately recognised Gay's political innuendo and were greatly amused by it. 'Bluff Bob' subsequently became a popular nickname for Walpole.

I. IV

5 he spends his Life among Women] An allusion to Walpole's love-life.

Walpole was married but he also maintained a mistress, Maria Skerrett (or Skerritt), and his adulterous relationship with her was public knowledge. After the death of his first wife in 1737, he married his mistress.

10 bitter bad] extremely bad, very biased.

11 the Camp] This has been glossed as 'transportation', but since Mrs Peachum is talking about 'matters of Death' and since the word was associated with army life (as it still is), the primary meaning is 'military service'. As has been pointed out in the Introduction, Gay draws a parallel between highwaymen and soldiers at several points in the play in order to establish how much they and their activities have in common. See, for example, I. VIII. 27–9, I. X. 12–4, II. I. 10–1 and II. III. 3–7.

13–20 *If any Wench . . . an* Adonis] The Roman Goddess of Love, Venus, like her Greek equivalent, Aphrodite, possessed a magic girdle that had the power of making its wearer extremely attractive and desirable. In Homer's *Iliad*, for example, Hera borrows Aphrodite's girdle in order to arouse the love of Zeus. Applied to faces 'smug' usually meant 'smooth', but the primary meaning of '*smuggly*' here is 'handsome' or 'attractive'. In the fifth line of the song, '*fit*' is a verb and '*so*' refers back to the wearing of Venus's girdle. '*Zone*' in the sixth line means 'girdle' or 'encircling band'. Mrs Peachum is therefore drawing an exact parallel between Venus's girdle and a hangman's noose. Just as a plain girl who wears the magic girdle is transformed into a kind of Venus, a common criminal with a rope around his neck becomes a kind of Adonis. The mythological connection between Venus and Adonis reinforces the parallel.

41 *Bagshot*] See the note on ROBIN OF BAGSHOT in the Commentary on the Dramatis Personae.

42 Party] game.

43 Quadrille] A four-handed card-game played with a pack of forty cards, the eights, nines and tens of the ordinary pack being discarded. During the 1720's quadrille began to replace ombre as the fashionable card-game and became extremely popular. In time, quadrille was itself superseded by whist.

45 *Mary-bone*] Marylebone Gardens, with its notorious gaming-houses, was London's gambling centre.

45 the Chocolate-houses] Gambling was a feature of London's chocolate-houses, which were essentially male preserves. They were also fashionable centres of social life where professional men, writers and members of the beau monde met casually to talk, argue and gossip while drinking chocolate.

46 Play] gambling.

71 a *Temple* Coffee-House] This would have been situated near the Inner Temple and the Middle Temple, two of London's four Inns of Court, and presumably would have catered mainly for lawyers and law students. Coffee-houses were identical to chocolate-houses (see last note but one) with the obvious exception that coffee was the drink served. An attraction at both were the pretty girls who worked at the bars, pouring the drinks.

79 matter] be concerned about.

81 to make herself a Property] Before the reforms of the nineteenth and twentieth centuries, a married woman had few legal rights. On marriage, everything a woman owned except for her personal effects was vested

in her husband, so that she did, in effect, become his possession or property. It is of course typical of Peachum that he should view human relationships in mercantile terms.

82–3 like a Court Lady to a Minister of State] This allusion to Walpole, who was a Court favourite, especially of Queen Caroline (George II's Queen), enhances the satirical parallel drawn between a criminal gang and senior government officials.

91 sift] question closely.

92 Cambric] fine white linen frequently used for handkerchiefs.

93 Chap] purchaser, dealer. (Abbreviation of 'Chapman'.)

I. V

7 Oar] A variant spelling of 'Ore' still used in the eighteenth century although much less common than the unambiguous 'Ore'.

10 try'd] refined, purified.

I. VI

4–5 cut the Rope of thy Life] The ironic pun on 'Rope'—it is the hangman's rope that is likely to 'cut the Rope' of Filch's life—may not be as obvious as it was before the abolition of capital punishment.

7 the Opera] The Opera House, otherwise known as the King's Theatre, was one of Vanbrugh's buildings and was situated in the Haymarket. It opened in 1705 as the Queen's Theatre—Anne was then on the throne—and subsequently became the home of Italian opera in London.

12 Redriff] Rotherhithe, a part of London's dockland on the south bank of the Thames, east of the Tower.

17 Fobs] small pockets in the waist-bands of breeches for watches, money or other valuables.

20 since I was pumpt] If a petty thief or pickpocket was caught in the act of stealing, his captors often provided their own rough-and-ready justice by pumping cold water over him for some time. In Trivia (III, 73–6) Gay himself describes the punishments sometimes administered to pickpockets:

Seiz'd by rough hands, he's
  dragg'd amid the rout,
And stretch'd beneath the pump's
  incessant spout:
Or plung'd in miry ponds, he
  gasping lies,
Mud choaks his mouth, and
  plaisters o'er his eyes.

20–1 taking up] This has been glossed as 'reforming', but the primary meaning is 'enlisting' (as a sailor).

22 Hockley in the Hole] The famous Bear Garden at Hockley-in-the-Hole in Clerkenwell was the scene of bear-baiting, bull-baiting, cock-fights, quarter-staff contests and various other sporting activities that provided entertainment for London's lower classes. Gay refers to it in Trivia (II, 407–12):

When through the town with slow
  and solemn air,
Led by the nostril, walks the
  muzled bear;
Behind him moves majestically
  dull,
The pride of Hockley-hole, the
  surly bull;
Learn hence the periods of the
  week to name,
Mondays and Thursdays are the
  days of game.

By far the most famous contemporary description of the Bear Garden is one of Steele's contributions to The

Spectator, No. 436 (21 July 1712). Gay's incongruous linking of 'Valour' with Hockley-in-the-Hole and the gaming-dens of Marylebone is typical of the complex irony of the play. It undermines the conventional conception of valour, but at the same time suggests that true valour is just as likely to be found among criminals as among aristocrats. Spoken by Mrs Peachum, this remark also exemplifies her absurd pretentions to respectability and gentility.

26 the *Old-Baily*] London's criminal court. (See Commentary on I. II. 38.)

30 the Ordinary's Paper] One of the principal duties of the Ordinary, the name given to the chaplain of Newgate Prison, was to prepare condemned prisoners for death. The Ordinary's Paper, which was published from time to time, was mainly devoted to his account of how some of the condemned spent their last hours and went to their deaths. The Ordinary also decided whether a prisoner on trial was entitled to 'benefit of clergy', which resulted in a reduced sentence, such as transportation instead of death. In the eighteenth century 'benefit of clergy' could be given only to literate first offenders convicted of less serious felonies. They had to read a passage from the Bible, usually the opening of Psalm 51 (known as the 'neck verse'), to the satisfaction of the Ordinary. Mrs Peachum is urging Filch to study his 'Book' (the Bible) so that he will qualify for 'benefit of clergy' when the time comes.

44 Cordial] strong sweet alcoholic drink used as a stimulant.

I. VII

3–4 an Assembly] The large-scale social function known as the public assembly was a regular feature of fashionable life in the eighteenth century at which people conversed, gossiped, danced and carried on amorous intrigues. The private assembly was more modest, in every sense of the word, and resembled a modern 'At Home' party.

13–6 *But, when once pluck'd . . . under feet*] Covent Garden was as notorious for its prostitutes as it was famous for its vegetable, fruit and flower market. In the vehicle of the metaphor, Covent Garden is the produce market to which the plucked flower is sent, but in the tenor of the metaphor, Covent Garden is the flesh-market to which the ex-virgin is sentenced by society. By the juxtaposition of Covent Garden, with its double meaning, and a natural garden, Polly's song expresses the poignancy of lost virginity and reveals the harshness of a social code that demanded the penalty of social ostracism for a girl who momentarily succumbed to her sexual desires.

I. VIII

6 *As Men should serve a Cowcumber, she flings herself away*] Cucumbers seem to have been regarded by some people as unsuitable for human consumption and fit only to be flung away. Boswell records Dr Johnson's comment that Gay's line 'has no waggish meaning, with reference to men flinging away cucumbers as too *cooling*, which some have thought; for it has been a common saying of physicians in England, that a cucumber should be well sliced, and dressed with pepper and vinegar, and then thrown out, as good for nothing' (*Life of Johnson*, ed. G. B. Hill (Oxford, 1950), vol. v, p. 289). Mrs Peachum is therefore

comparing her daughter's behaviour to this elaborate yet futile preparation of a cucumber. (See Robert S. Hunting's short article listed in the Bibliography.)

30 getting] growing richer.

32 are you ruin'd or no] A particularly interesting example of the semantic inversions that pervade the play. 'Ruined' was the word normally used to describe a girl who had lost her virginity pre-maritally, but in Peachum's mouth it means 'married', the exact opposite of the usual sense. (See also I. IV. 90.)

36–7 I'll make you plead by squeezing out an Answer from you] An allusion to the legal torture of 'pressing', officially known as *peine forte et dure*. Defendants who refused to plead either guilty or not guilty were pressed under heavy weights in an attempt to force a plea from them. If they did not submit, they were pressed to death. The reason why men, especially wealthy men, sometimes chose this agonising death was to safeguard the interests of their wives and families. In addition to being executed, a prisoner convicted of a felony forfeited his entire estate, and his family was consequently beggared. However, a man who refused to plead could not be convicted, and although he himself died, he had the satisfaction of knowing that his family was secure. *Peine forte et dure* was still in use during Gay's lifetime but was discontinued before the middle of the eighteenth century.

82 nice] particular.

108 Repeating-Watch] watch that struck the hours and the quarters and also repeated the previous chime whenever required.

110 *Drury-Lane*] The Drury Lane district was the main centre of prostitution in London. The famous passage about prostitutes in *Trivia* (III, 259–306) opens:

> O! may thy virtue guard thee through the roads
> Of *Drury*'s mazy courts, and dark abodes,
> The harlots guileful paths, who nightly stand,
> Where *Katherine-street* descends into the *Strand*.

112 *Tunbridge*] Tunbridge Wells in Kent, with its medicinal springs, was one of the chief resorts of London Society in the eighteenth century and consequently attracted thieves and pickpockets from the capital.

I. IX

7 Fuller's Earth] Fulling was a process in which fabrics were scoured and thickened by being moistened, heated and pressed. Fullers used a special kind of earth containing hydrous aluminium silicate to clean the fabric. Gay's figurative use of the words is unusual and effective.

I. X

18 Jointure] legal arrangement for the joint-holding of property by husband and wife, very often made as a means of providing for the woman in case of widowhood.

30 peach'd] brought to trial (by informing against).

40 nick'd] hit precisely (nick'd the Matter: hit the nail on the head).

46 *Depends*] This pun was obvious to Gay's contemporaries because the meaning 'hang down' or 'be suspended' was still current in the eighteenth century.

52 *Turtle*] The turtle-dove is a

traditional symbol of conjugal affection and constancy.

60 particular] devoted to one person.

I. XI

o s.d. P O L L Y *listning*] Although Polly leaves her parents at the end of I. x, she remains in view of the audience throughout I. XI, during which she eavesdrops on the conversation.

6–7 Stratagem] cunning, ingenuity.

I. XII

Although Polly's anguished soliloquy is much more thàn burlesque, it does illustrate the verbal burlesque of Augustan 'sentimental drama' that Gay includes in the play. Polly reflects on her predicament in a similar way to the distraught heroines of Rowe's 'she-tragedies' and other contemporary plays, expressing her fears in the inflated language of 'sentimental drama'. The resulting incongruity between 'low' matter and 'elevated' manner ridicules the self-conscious pathos of 'sentimental' heroines and the overwrought emotionalism of 'sentimental drama'. Yet put in the mouth of Polly, Gay's burlesque of false emotion becomes an expression of real emotion and genuine pathos. As in other parts of the play, he achieves an extraordinary fusion of laughter and tears.

2 the Nosegay in his Hand] Condemned criminals on their way to the gallows were presented with nosegays at St Sepulchre's, the church near Newgate.

4 the Windows of *Holborn*] On their way to execution at Tyburn, condemned prisoners were taken through the streets of London in an open cart, the route being from New-gate along Holborn and Tyburn Road (now Oxford Street) to near where Marble Arch now stands. The cart paused at an ale-house in the parish of St Giles-in-the-Fields for the prisoners to take their last drink. As Polly's premonition indicates, an execution was a public event with large crowds usually turning out to watch both the last journey of the criminals and their deaths. Public executions were intended to fill the condemned with guilt and shame so that the spectacle of their deaths would deter others from crime, but they actually provided a kind of entertainment, often taking on an almost carnival spirit with the criminals playing the parts of heroes. As a result condemned prisoners were frequently pitied, admired and glorified, as in the case of Jack Sheppard, on whom Macheath is partly based. In *An Enquiry into the Causes of the Late Increase of Robbers* (1751), Henry Fielding argued that the executions at Tyburn were more of an encouragement to crime than a deterrent, and he advocated the introduction of much more solemn and private executions outside the Old Bailey immediately after sentence had been passed.

5 the Tree] The gallows at Tyburn, usually known as Tyburn Tree, probably stood at what is now the junction of Edgware Road and Bayswater Road, although some authorities think that Connaught Square was the site.

6 *Jack Ketch*] The original Jack Ketch was an executioner and public hangman in London from about 1663 until his death in 1686, except for a brief period at the beginning of 1686 when he was replaced for offending the Sheriffs of London. What made him notorious was the clumsy way in

which he carried out the beheadings of Lord Russell (1683) and the Duke of Monmouth (1685), two of the most important political prisoners of the period. His name was given to the hangman in the puppet play *Punchinello*, introduced from Italy shortly after his death, and was subsequently applied to his successors as a nickname until well into the nineteenth century.

11 Conversation] company (including sexual intimacy).

I. XIII

Verbal burlesque of 'sentimental drama' continues in this scene with ridicule of the typical hero's declarations of everlasting love for the heroine and of the tearful separation scenes in which hero and heroine talk about the impossibility of parting. Like I. XII, this scene nevertheless transcends burlesque to achieve true pathos.

31–3 Greenland's *Coast . . . eternal Frost*] Compare *Trivia* (III, 401–2):

> . . . or shiv'ring crost
> Dark *Greenland*'s mountains of eternal frost[.]

69 S.D. *he at one Door, she at the other*] Two proscenium doors with balconies above them, one at each side of the stage, were standard features of Restoration and eighteenth century theatre design.

II. I

4 so clever a made] such a well-made.
5 fleaing] (*a*) flaying (*b*) cheating, extorting money from people.
6 Otamys] skeletons.
6 *Surgeon's   Hall*] The Barber-Surgeons' Hall, situated in Monkwell Street, had been used for anatomy

demonstrations since the middle of the sixteenth century. The Charter of the Company of Barbers and Surgeons approved by Parliament in 1540 granted the use of four bodies of executed felons annually for this purpose, and many subsequent specimens were hanged criminals, like Matt of the Mint's brother Tom whose 'Accident' was clearly caused by the rope. It was not until 1745 that the Barbers and the Surgeons separated into two distinct Companies with the Barbers retaining the old Hall in Monkwell Street and the Surgeons building new premises near Newgate. Towards the end of the century the Company of Surgeons moved to a house in Lincoln's Inn Fields more or less on the site of the present College, and in 1800 the Company was reconstituted as the Royal College of Surgeons. The Barber-Surgeons' Hall was destroyed during the Second World War but has since been rebuilt.

II. II

42 *Moor-fields*] A disreputable district of London, north of the old City walls.
43 S.H. March in *Rinaldo*] This tune is taken from Handel's first opera for the English stage. *Rinaldo*, based on the story of Rinaldo and Armida in Tasso's *Gerusalemme Liberata*, was composed to a libretto by Rossi at the request of Aaron Hill, the manager of the Queen's Theatre in the Haymarket, shortly after Handel's arrival in England in 1710. The first production took place in 1711. In the opera the March is purely instrumental.
48–51 *See the Ball . . . to Gold*] By means of this ingenious conceit, Matt of the Mint compares the relative

achievements of highwaymen and alchemists (*Chymists*) in transmuting base metals into gold. Whereas the alchemist labours fruitlessly over his alembic and cauldron, the highwayman employs fire in the form of gunfire and lead in the form of balls or round bullets in order to obtain gold by the simpler method of stealing it.

II. III

1   *Polly* is most confoundedly bit] In this context 'bit' is ambiguous, depending on whether it is understood to refer back to 'Fool' or to 'fond' in the preceding sentence. The primary meaning is 'deceived', the sense being that Polly is completely wrong in believing Macheath to be as faithful to her as she is to him. As Macheath goes on to explain, he is devoted to women rather than to any one woman. But 'bit' can also refer to 'fond Wench', the sense being that Polly has been badly bitten by love and is love-struck.

6–7   *Drury-Lane*] See Commentary on I. VIII. 110.

20   so strong a Cordial] so invigorating a stimulant.

24   *Vinegar Yard*] A haunt of prostitutes just off Drury Lane.

25   *Lewkner's Lane*] Another haunt of prostitutes near Drury Lane in which Jonathan Wild had run a brothel.

II. IV

2   Quality] i.e. 'women of quality'; high society women.

3   Paint] make-up.

10   Strong-Waters] alcoholic spirits.

20   Tally-men] people who sold goods on credit, especially clothes to prostitutes.

22   Turtle] turtle-dove, here signifying amorousness.

23–4   *If Musick be the Food of Love, play on*] The opening line of Shakespeare's *Twelfth Night*, spoken by Orsino.

24   E'er] A variant spelling of 'Ere' sometimes used in the eighteenth century although strictly speaking erroneous since 'E'er' is really a contraction of 'Ever'.

26   the *French* Tune] The music that follows, 'Cotillon', is French.

26 s.D.   *A Dance a la ronde in the French Manner*] Gay must have intended this dance of Macheath and the whores in the tavern to be a parody of the dignified and formal ballet dancing often incorporated in Italian opera.

55   Lutestring] glossy silk fabric.

55   Padesoy] strong-corded silk fabric.

59   nick'd] robbed.

63   fine Parts] artful qualities, cunning.

88   in keeping] kept as a mistress.

101   bating] leaving aside.

106   bleed] part with money.

106–7   I have sent . . . the Plantations] By making the apprentices 'bleed freely' (spend money like water) and so live beyond their means in order to keep her as a mistress, Mrs Vixen has forced them to resort to theft. On conviction, they have been transported.

115   *Souse*] sou, small coin of little value.

119   These] Macheath's pistols, as the subsequent stage-direction makes clear.

126   I must and will have a Kiss] Possibly a mock-heroic allusion to Judas Iscariot's kiss of betrayal that led to Christ's arrest. (See Commentary on III. VI. 74–5 for another possible parallel to the events preceding the Crucifixion.)

II. V

4 Whores] William Empson (see Bibliography) has drawn attention to this interesting 'double irony'. Although 'Whores' is the climax of Macheath's string of insults, it is also, paradoxically, the literal truth since the women he is addressing are prostitutes. Several times in the preceding scene Macheath calls them 'Ladies', so that when he actually uses 'Whores' he cuts through the pretences he has maintained before their betrayal of him to Peachum. There is also the implication that all women are untrustworthy and so no better than whores.

5 particular] exceptional.

II. VII

D.P. *Turnkeys*] jailors, warders.

3 Garnish, Captain, Garnish] The 'garnish' was the customary payment made by prisoners or extorted from them when they entered prison. It went either to the jailors or to their fellow-prisoners or to both. This practice continued throughout the eighteenth century but was eventually banned in the early nineteenth century. Macheath's complaint later in this scene about the fees at Newgate being 'so many, and so exorbitant' had a lot of truth in it, because going to prison could be a very expensive business. Prisons were in private hands and were run as commercial enterprises, fees being charged for providing various services and comforts. Although legal, this practice was grossly abused, especially as the poorly paid prison-staff needed to supplement their meagre incomes.

19 nicest] most refined, most fastidious.

II. VIII

4 *Basilisk*] mythical creature (hatched by a reptile from the egg of an old cock) whose gaze and breath were fatal.

II. IX

49–50 the Ordinary] See Commentary on I. VI. 30.

II. X

The quarrel between Peachum and Lockit in this scene is based on that between Brutus and Cassius in Shakespeare's *Julius Caesar* (IV. III), but it has often been argued that the famous quarrel between Walpole and his brother-in-law Charles Townshend at Colonel Selwyn's home in Cleveland Court provided Gay with another model. Like Walpole, Lord Townshend (1674–1738) was a Minister of State and one of the most influential political figures at the time. Accounts of the dispute between the two politicians, as in William Coxe's *Memoirs of the Life and Administration of Sir Robert Walpole, Earl of Orford* (London, 1798; vol. I, pp. 335–6), certainly bear a close resemblance to this scene. At the height of their quarrel, for example, Walpole and Townshend are said to have collared each other in the same way that Peachum and Lockit do. However, this particular argument between the two politicians did not take place until 1729 and could not therefore have been a source for this scene, as Jean B. Kern has shown (see Bibliography; pp. 97–8 of Oswald Doughty's edition—'30' in the Bibliography—provide another interesting discussion of this issue). Kern suggests that since some time elapsed between the quarrel in 1729 and the writing of the various Memoirs in which it is recorded, the dispute in the play may have become confused with the actual quarrel. In other words, the writers of the Memoirs may to some extent have based their accounts of the argument between Walpole and Townshend on this scene. Nevertheless the repeated use of 'Brother' by Peachum and Lockit does refer to the relationship between Walpole and Townshend, and this scene undoubtedly satirises the two most prominent Whigs of the day. Differences between Walpole and Townshend had been evident since 1725, and Gay is making satirical capital out of the growing tension and enmity between them.

7   This long Arrear of the Government] i.e. 'These long-standing arrears of payment by the Government' (of the £40 rewards for the evidence supplied by Peachum and Lockit that has led to the conviction and subsequent execution of criminals).

26   *Ned Clincher*'s Name] In contemporary slang a 'clincher' was a person noted for witty repartee, especially a punster. In the slang of the underworld 'clinch' meant 'condemned cell'. One of Swift's best-known poems is 'Clever Tom Clinch going to be hanged', written shortly before *The Beggar's Opera* in 1726 or 1727. With its reference to Jonathan Wild—'My honest Friend *Wild*'—and its comparison of the criminal to the hero—Tom Clinch 'hung like a Hero'—this short poem has affinities with Gay's play, and it is quite likely that Gay knew it.

28   Hold] cell.

59   nimm'd] stole.

II. XI

20   *e'er*] See Commentary on II. IV. 24.

II. XII

7   Perquisite] money given or received as a bribe.

II. XIII

15   *for th' Event*] This phrase is ambiguous. It could mean 'because of what has happened'—the swallow trapped behind the sash-window (Macheath put behind bars). But since 'the event' was sometimes used for 'the course of events', the phrase could mean 'while awaiting the outcome'.

18   S.D.   *Aside*] In the original text, this is placed between the two sentences that constitute Macheath's speech, but it refers only to the first. The second is spoken aloud in an attempt to pacify Lucy.

20   bilk'd] cheated.

39–42   *How happy . . . I say*] This song contains an obvious satirical comment on Walpole's relationships with his wife and his mistress. (See Commentary on I. IV. 5.) Throughout the play Gay makes the triangle of Macheath, Polly and Lucy reflect on the well-known triangle of Walpole, Lady Walpole and Maria Skerrett.

52   *bubbled*] deceived.

55   *bit*] deceived.

52–9   *I'm bubbled . . . I'm bubbled, &c*] The duets in the play are in one sense mock-duets, burlesquing the duets of Italian opera. This song is a particularly good example because the vocal line alternates between Polly and Lucy in a very similar way to operatic duets—those of Dorinda and Angelica, both of whom love the

African prince Medoro, in Handel's *Orlando* provide a useful comparison. Equally good examples are two duets sung by Polly and Lucy in Act III, Airs XLIX and LII.

60 Fetch] trick.

74 *trapan*] beguile.

94–103 *Why how now . . . Saucy Jade*] In this song '*Dirt*' (96) and '*made*' (101) are sung as operatic melismata with each word running for nearly three bars of music. These are the only extended melismata in the play, in which one note of music usually corresponds to one syllable. Considering that the struggle between Polly and Lucy over Macheath alludes to the professional rivalry between Faustina and Cuzzoni (see Commentary on the Introduction 18–20), the bravura singing reinforces Gay's satire of the two feuding sopranos.

III. I

8–9 I wish I may be burnt] This probably refers to the 'burning in the hand' or branding of convicted first offenders who escaped the death sentence by receiving 'benefit of clergy'. (See Commentary on I. VI. 30.) A letter 'T', signifying Tyburn, was branded on the base of the right thumb. But it could also refer to the burning to death of women convicted of high or petty treason, a form of execution that survived until 1790. Although responsible for freeing Macheath, Lucy plays the innocent and claims that she deserves to be 'burnt' if she is not telling the truth.

24 *score*] record debts, keep an account of drinks served.

38 Bubbles] fools (are their own Bubbles: make fools of themselves, deceive themselves).

III. II

2 is leaky in his Liquor] (*a*) talks freely, gives away secrets, under the influence of alcohol (*b*) urinates frequently when drinking.

16 *fail of a Chap*] are without a customer, lack a victim.

18–9 *Like Pikes . . . their Friends*] The simile is very appropriate, because these scavenger fresh-water fish are noted for their voracity.

23 Quartern] quarter of a pint.

III. III

1–2 like a shotten Herring] Lockit's simile of a herring that has spawned to describe the emaciated Filch is very appropriate, because the reason for Filch's wasted appearance is the excessive sexual intercourse he has been having with female prisoners so that they can 'plead their bellies' at their trials. (See Commentary on I. II. 4.)

4 thorough] A variant spelling of 'through'.

9 tip off] die.

III. IV

4 meer] A variant spelling of 'mere'.

22–3 One Man . . . a Hedge] i.e. 'Whereas some men can commit crimes with impunity, others are regarded with suspicion even when behaving innocently.' The contrast is between influential people in high society and in the Government and their moral counterparts in low society, thieves and highwaymen.

24 Mechanics] low people. (A term of contempt for manual workers.)

28 deep Play] gambling with a great deal of money at stake.

30 Setting] setting upon, holding up.

38 *Rouleau*] cylindrical packet or roll

of gold coins (in this case the property of 'the Money-Lenders' who
lent money to gamblers in the
gaming-houses at extortionate rates
of interest).

44 nick'd] This could simply mean
'cheated', presumably at the gaming-
table. However, in the dice-game of
Hazard a 'nick' was a winning throw,
so that Macheath could mean that the
'Man of Distinction' has won a great
deal of money from him at Hazard
by throwing 'nicks' more often than
Macheath himself. If this is the meaning, there may be an implication of
cheating although this is not necessarily the case.

III. V

1 The Coronation Account] The
Coronation of George II took place
on 11 October 1727. The 'Account'
is of things stolen during the cele-
brations.

5 Instalments] The annual installations
of the Lord Mayors of London. An
'Instalment' provided a field-day for
robbers and pickpockets, but from
what Peachum says about George
II's Coronation being worth 'above
ten Instalments', Coronation Day in
1727 must have been a thieves'
paradise.

7 Lady's Tail] train of a woman's
dress.

8 Tally-woman] See Commentary on
II. IV. 20.

9 trick out] fit out.

10 going into Keeping] becoming
mistresses.

16 Pockets] pocket-books, purses.

22 Bring us then more Liquor]
Although there is no stage-direction
here, these words are obviously
spoken to a servant, either on-stage
or off-stage, who brings the 'Liquor'
and then leaves so as to be able to
make the entry necessary later in this
scene.

26 Gudgeons] (a) small fresh-water
fish that are very easy to catch (b)
gullible people, fools.

33 Grate] cage.

37-8 Correspondence] relations (keep a
good Correspondence together: keep
on good terms).

III. VI

3 curious in] particular about.

13 Mantoes] loose gowns worn by
women.

14 Chap] See Commentary on I. IV.
93.

22 The Act for destroying the Mint]
An Act of Parliament (9, George I,
C.28) was passed during the 1722–3
Session to bring 'more effectual
Execution of Justice in a pretended
privileged Place in the Parish of
Saint George in the County of
Surrey, commonly called the Mint;
and for bringing to speedy and
exemplary Justice such Offenders
as are therein mentioned; and for
giving Relief to such Persons as are
proper Objects of Charity and Compassion there'. (See The Statutes at
Large (London, 1758), vol. IV, pp.
463–5.) The Act came into force
after 10 October 1723. Earlier
attempts to enforce the law in 'the
Mint', a notorious part of Southwark
used as a place of refuge by debtors
and criminals and commonly thought
to be beyond the reach of the law,
had not proved successful.

23 stept out of the way] As a tally-
woman, Mrs Trapes provides clothes
on credit to her customers, who are
prostitutes. This phrase is
ambiguous, both the literal and
metaphorical meanings being applicable. Metaphorically, it is equivalent
to 'stepped out of line', and in this

context means 'did not keep up her payments'. The literal meaning is that Mrs Trapes's defaulting customers avoided her or kept out of her way.

27–8   the Act too against Imprisonment for small Sums] A measure (12, George I, C.29) passed by Parliament during the 1725–6 Session 'to prevent frivolous and vexatious Arrests', especially for small debts. Under the provisions of the Act, which took effect from 24 June 1726, 'no Person shall be held to Special Bail upon any Process issuing out of any Superior Court, where the Cause of Action shall not amount to the Sum of ten Pounds or upwards; nor out of any Inferior Court, where the Cause of Action shall not amount to the Sum of forty Shillings or upwards'. (See *The Statutes at Large* (London, 1758), vol. IV, pp. 562–3.)

29–30   when a Lady can borrow . . . Hank upon her] Here 'borrow' means 'obtain on credit', so that Mrs Trapes is complaining that since the new Act came into force she has no way of making her customers pay her what they owe her because she can no longer use the threat of the Debtors' Prison. Previously she had had this 'Hank upon' (hold over) them.

44   bilking of] cheating.

45   eleven fine Customers now down under the Surgeon's Hands] The whores are presumably being treated for venereal disease. (See Commentary on I. II. 27–8.) If they were confined for childbirth as has been suggested, they would be under the care of a midwife, not a surgeon.

74–5   so whatever happens, I wash my Hands on't] Possibly a mock-heroic allusion to Pontius Pilate's washing his hands of responsibility for Christ's fate.

III. VII

11   I have the Rats-bane ready] Prison scenes involving cups of poison occurred regularly in Italian opera at this time, as Bertrand H. Bronson has shown (see Bibliography). Several operas composed by Handel in the decade before *The Beggar's Opera*, including *Radamisto* (1720) and *Tamerlano* (1724), contain such scenes, which are usually very emotional and highly dramatic. Lucy's determined attempt to poison Polly, which she announces here and which continues until the end of III. x, burlesques these operatic scenes. The satirical parallel is strongly emphasised in III. x when Polly drops the poisoned 'Cup of Strong-Waters' without having touched the contents. In Italian opera the poisoned cup is usually spilled before anyone can drink from it.

11–3   I can lay her Death . . . in Question] After the Glorious Revolution of 1688, trade with France was suspended and the importing of French spirits prohibited. As a result the recently discovered and very cheap Dutch drink of geneva or gin became extremely popular. ('Gin' is an abbreviation of 'geneva', the anglicised form of the Dutch word.) By the time Gay wrote the play, the annual consumption in England was about five million gallons. Gin shops mushroomed, especially in and around London, but the spirit could be obtained at many ordinary shops as well and even on the streets from pedlars with barrows. Much of the gin was of poor quality so that it was literally poisonous, and sudden deaths in gin shops were not infrequent. In 1736 the so-called Gin Act was introduced by Sir Joseph

Jekyll with Walpole's support to curb the ready availability of crude gin, but this severe excise measure encountered so much hostility that it could not be fully implemented.

III. VIII

3 the Spleen] bad-temper and low spirits. The spleen had been thought to be the seat of anger and melancholy. In the eighteenth century the word was used to denote psychological states of moroseness, irritability, dejection and sullenness. References to the spleen abound in contemporary literature, the two most famous treatments being the Cave of Spleen in Canto IV of Pope's *The Rape of the Lock* (1714) and Matthew Green's *The Spleen* (1737).

8 *Vapours*] ill humour, especially depression, supposedly caused by exhalations from the bodily organs. It was essentially a female condition.

48 particular] devoted to one person.

62 a Cup too low] (*a*) in need of a drink (*b*) depressed.

68 *chirping*] cheering.

III. XI

John O. Rees (see Bibliography) suggests that in this scene Gay may have intended a mock-heroic comparison between Macheath and Hercules. The classical myth known as the Judgment of Hercules about Hercules's difficult choice between two goddesses, Virtue and Vice (or Pleasure), was widely used by European poets and painters from the Renaissance to the eighteenth century as an allegory or icon of a universal moral dilemma. According to Rees, Macheath's dilemma when faced with both Polly and Lucy (especially in Air LIII) is a burlesque version of the Judgment of Hercules, with Polly playing the part of Virtue and Lucy that of Vice. In his eagerness to establish as close a parallel as possible, Rees overstates his case and therefore nearly destroys it. He describes Lucy as 'vicious' and argues that 'Polly and Lucy have become theatrical prototypes of good and evil', obviously equivalent to the two goddesses in the myth, but this is totally unfair to Lucy as she is presented in this scene. Lucy's attempt to poison Polly in the scenes immediately preceding III. XI may make her resemble 'the stage villainess' as Rees claims, but at the end of III. X she expresses relief that her plan has failed, and in III. XI her main concern, like Polly's, is to save Macheath from the hangman. Gay can hardly have intended such a close parallel to the Judgment of Hercules as Rees maintains, but considering the mock-heroic comparisons between Macheath and 'the great Heroes' elsewhere—both Polly (I. XIII. 16) and Peachum (II. v. 5–6) speak of him as one—it is possible that Gay had the myth in mind. As Hogarth's famous painting (now in the Tate Gallery) of an early performance of this scene makes particularly clear, the characters are symmetrically arranged in the form of a tableau resembling pictorial representations of the Judgment of Hercules. Peachum and Polly are on one side of the central figure, Macheath, and Lockit and Lucy on the other. Even the action is symmetrically patterned with each girl appealing first to Macheath to acknowledge her love and then to her father to spare Macheath's life. The symmetry is further reinforced by the way in which both Polly's and Lucy's songs to their fathers, Airs

LIV and LV, end with the word 'May'.

28 *Which way shall I turn me?—How can I decide?*] Macheath's words echo Antony's 'O Dolabella, which way shall I turn?' when he is torn between love and honour in Act III of Dryden's heroic tragedy, *All for Love*. Like Macheath, Antony is trying to decide between his mistress (Cleopatra) and his wife (Octavia), but Dryden's treatment of his hero's dilemma is deeply serious and highly emotional. In presenting a similar situation in comic terms, Gay incidentally burlesques one of the most famous scenes in contemporary tragedy.

64 *Fry*] small fry.

III. XII

2 particular] precise, detailed.

10 S.D. *A Dance of Prisoners in Chains*] This grotesque dance, like the dance of Macheath and the whores in II. IV, burlesques operatic ballet.

III. XIII

Although the Beggar claims in the Introduction that there is 'no Recitative' in his opera, Macheath's sung soliloquy in this scene is, amongst other things, a burlesque of operatic recitative. Excluding the final Air (LXVII), which is more like a culminating aria, the words of the monologue are set to music from no less than nine well-known songs so that there is a constantly changing melodic line, resembling the vocal fluctuations of Italian recitative.

6 *Brimmer*] glass filled to the brim.

20 *Busses*] kisses.

26–9 *But Gold . . .* Tyburn *Tree*] Compare *Newgate's Garland* (3–4):

Ye Sharpers so rich, who can buy off the Noose,
Ye honester poor Rogues, who die in your Shoes[.]

III. XIV

3 peach] inform against, betray.

III. XV

3–4 Ship yourselves off for the *West-Indies*] The seeds of Gay's sequel to *The Beggar's Opera*, *Polly*, which is set in the West Indies, are present in this remark. White women were in very short supply in the colonies.

9–20 *Would I might . . . the Bell*] The high point of many Italian operas occurs in the closing scenes when the protagonists are brought together to sing a fairly complex trio, quartet or quintet, depending on the number of protagonists. This song, the only trio in the play, is at one level a burlesque imitation of operatic climaxes. In earlier scenes, Polly, Lucy and Macheath are on stage together for some time, and Polly and Lucy even sing two duets in his presence, but it is only at the 'tragic climax' that all three sing together. The unheroic and ungallant but decidedly human behaviour of Gay's 'hero' adds much to the burlesque effect of this mock-trio. Gay's choice of tune for this song about hanging is very appropriate, 'All you that must take a Leap' being a ballad about the execution of two criminals.

20 *the Toll of the Bell*] The largest bell of St Sepulchre's Church, near Newgate, began to toll shortly before condemned prisoners were taken from the Prison to be executed. In Restoration and Augustan tragedy, a tolling bell at the approaching death of the hero seems to have been a very reliable theatrical

device for arousing pity and terror. The most famous example occurs at the end of Otway's very popular *Venice Preserv'd*, in which a passing-bell tolls as Pierre's execution becomes imminent. Gay here incorporates a burlesque of the device, and he almost certainly had Otway's play in mind. Pierre's words as he and Jaffeir ascend the scaffold, 'Come, now I'm ready', are echoed comically by Macheath at the end of this scene. *Venice Preserv'd* is the main target of Gay's burlesque of contemporary tragedy in *The What D'Ye Call It*.

21 s.p. CHORUS] The composition of this chorus is not clear. Of the five occasions on which Gay specifies a chorus, this is the only one that is not a crowd scene. Macheath's gang sing as a chorus in the tavern scenes (Airs XIX and XX) as do the whores (Air XXII), and the entire cast join in Air LXIX at the very end of the play. It has been suggested that this chorus is really a trio consisting of the on-stage characters, Polly, Lucy and Macheath, but it is more likely that Gay intended an off-stage chorus producing a bell-like effect, the tolling that Macheath hears.

24 four Wives more] The scenes in which a wife or mistress visits her condemned husband or lover are among the most emotionally indulgent in Italian opera and in Augustan 'sentimental drama'. In his prison scenes, such as II. XIII and III. XI, Gay ridicules such sentimental episodes by introducing two 'wives' instead of one and developing the situation accordingly, but for a final attack he increases the number of 'wives' in the condemned cell to six. His burlesque method is to inject into a stock situation of opera and 'sentimental drama' a commonplace of

farce—the scene in which a philanderer or rake is simultaneously confronted by the two or more women he has married or been having affairs with. Furthermore, by providing each of the four women with a child, Gay burlesques another sentimental feature of contemporary plays—the introduction of innocent children at critical moments and in scenes of pathos.

III. XVI

The surprise ending that rescues Macheath from the gallows and that results from the intervention of the Beggar and the Player is in one way not a surprise, because a tragic conclusion to the play is inconceivable considering its essentially comic nature. Gay accomplishes several things simultaneously in this scene. He combines direct condemnation of Italian opera with burlesque of the arbitrary methods employed in opera to achieve a happy ending. In doing this he also ridicules 'the Taste of the Town', implying not only that the public is indifferent to his serious moral purpose but also that their lack of taste is symptomatic of debased moral standards, indeed of the immoral forces exposed and attacked in the play. The contemporary political significance of Macheath's escape from death has already been discussed in the Introduction (see page 17). A similar reversal of fortune occurs near the end of *The What D'Ye Call It*. Like Macheath, Peascod is under sentence of death but is saved by a last-minute reprieve. Gay's purpose in rescuing the essentially good Peascod is to ridicule the melodramatic revelations used in 'sentimental drama' to ensure poetic justice.

21-4 Had the Play . . . punish'd for

them] Although the Beggar's preceding remarks succinctly sum up
the social satire of the play, this final
statement about his original didactic
purpose is so deliberately ludicrous
in the context of the play that it must
be interpreted as burlesque of the
explicit moralising with which 'sentimental' plays almost invariably
close. It is also one of Gay's most
incisive ironies.

III. XVII

8–10 And for Life . . . own Secret] In
the original text the only stage-direction for these lines, indicating an
aside to Polly, is placed at the end of
Macheath's speech, so that it is not
clear how much of the speech it
applies to. The first and third of
these three sentences are addressed
to Polly alone because he would not
want any of her rivals to hear him
acknowledge her as his true wife. The
second sentence, 'As for the rest',
could also be spoken to Polly, if it is
taken to be equivalent to a dismis-
sive shrug of the shoulders indicating
that 'the rest of them' mean nothing
to him. But it is more likely that these
words are addressed to the assembled
company—'the rest of you'—and
mean that everyone should follow his
example by taking a partner and
joining in the dance. Gay's use of
dashes to separate the three sentences
supports this interpretation.

BIBLIOGRAPHY

I. Editions of 'The Beggar's Opera'

Editions of the play are legion. The following list is not complete, but includes all those I have consulted, twenty-five from the eighteenth century and twenty-five from the twentieth century. The really important eighteenth century editions are the three authorised London editions published before Gay's death in 1732 (1, 2, and 6 below). The other editions published before his death were pirated (3, 4, 5, and 7). The best modern editions are those by G. C. Faber, George H. Nettleton and Arthur E. Case, and Edgar V. Roberts (36, 44, and 49), although the facsimile of the Third Edition (London, 1729) is also important (46). Edward J. Dent's edition (45), being a vocal score of his arrangement of the music, does not provide a complete text, but I include it here because it differs from most musical adaptations, such as Frederic Austin's or Benjamin Britten's, in containing an Introduction that is of interest to a student of drama as well as to a musician.

(1) First Edition. London (Watts) 1728. (2) Second Edition. London (Watts) 1728. (3) First Edition. Dublin (Risk, Ewing and Smith) 1728. (4) Third Edition. Dublin (Risk, Ewing and Smith) 1728. (5) Third Edition. London 1728. A piracy issued under the forged imprint of John Watts. (6) Third Edition. London (Watts) 1729. (7) Fourth Edition. Dublin (Risk, Ewing and Smith) 1732. (8) Third Edition. London (Watts) 1733. (9) Fourth Edition. London (Watts) 1735. (10) Fifth Edition. London (Watts) 1742. (11) Seventh Edition. London 1745. A piracy. (12) Sixth Edition. London (Watts) 1749. (13) Sixth Edition. Dublin (Risk, Ewing and Smith) 1749. (14) Sixth Edition. Dublin (Dalton) 1749. (15) Glasgow (Foulis) 1753. (16) Seventh Edition. London (Watts) 1754. (17) in *Plays written by Mr. John Gay.* London (Tonson) 1760. (18) Edinburgh (Donaldson) 1760. (19) London (Tonson) 1761. (20) London (Tonson) 1765. (21) in *The Works of Mr. John Gay* (4 vols.). Dublin (Potts) 1770. (22) London (Strahan, Lowndes, Caslon, Griffin, Nicoll, Bladon and Kearsley) 1771. (23) in *The Works of Mr. John Gay* (4 vols.). London (Strahan and many others) 1772. (24) in *Plays written by Mr. John Gay.* London (Strahan, Lowndes, Caslon, Griffin, Nicoll, Bladon and Kearsley) 1772. (25) in *The Poetical, Dramatic, and Miscellaneous Works of John Gay* (6 vols.). London (Jeffery) 1795. (26) ed. G. H. Macleod. London (Moring: De La More Press) 1905. (27) in *Representative English Dramas from Dryden to Sheridan,* ed. F. Tupper and J. W. Tupper. New York (Oxford U.P.) 1914. (28) London (Secker) 1920. (29) London (Heinemann) 1921. (30) ed. O. Doughty. London (O'Connor) 1922. (31) in *The Plays of John Gay* (2 vols.). London (Chapman and Dodd) 1923. (32) in *Types of English Drama: 1660–1780,* ed. D. H. Stevens. Boston (Ginn) 1923. (33) with *Polly.* London (Chapman and Dodd) 1923. (34) London and Glasgow (Gowans and Gray) 1923. (35) London (Holerth Press) 1924. (36) in *The Poetical Works of John Gay,* ed. G. C. Faber. London (Oxford U.P.) 1926. (37) in *Eighteenth-Century Plays,* ed. J. Hampden. London (Dent) and New York (Dutton) 1928. Reprinted as

John Gay's The Beggar's Opera and other Eighteenth-Century Plays. (38) in *Eighteenth Century Comedy*, ed. W. D. Taylor. London (Oxford U.P.) 1929. (39) in *British Plays from the Restoration to 1820* (vol. II), ed. M. J. Moses. Boston (Little, Brown) 1929. (40) in *Plays of the Restoration and Eighteenth Century*, ed. D. MacMillan and H. M. Jones. London (Allen and Unwin) 1931. (41) ed. F. W. Bateson. London (Dent) 1934. (42) in *English Plays 1660–1820*, ed. A. E. Morgan. New York and London (Harper) 1935. (43) in *Twelve Famous Plays of the Restoration and Eighteenth Century*, ed. C. A. Moore. London (Penguin Books) 1937. (44) in *British Dramatists from Dryden to Sheridan*, ed. G. H. Nettleton and A. E. Case. Boston (Houghton Mifflin) 1939. Revised by G. W. Stone, 1969. (45) ed. E. J. Dent. London (Oxford U.P.) 1954. (46) Facsimile of the Third Edition (London, 1729) with commentaries by L. Kronenberger and M. Goberman. Larchmont, N.Y. (Argonaut Books) 1961. (47) in *Six Eighteenth-Century Plays*, ed. J. H. Wilson. Boston (Houghton Mifflin) 1963. (48) with Companion Pieces, ed. C. F. Burgess. New York (Appleton-Century-Crofts) 1966. (49) ed. E. V. Roberts. Lincoln, Neb. (U. of Nebraska P.) 1968 and London (Arnold) 1969. (50) in *Eighteenth Century Comedy*, ed. S. Trussler. London (Oxford U.P.) 1969. A new version of 38.

II. Related Studies

A. GENERAL

Armens, S. M. *John Gay, Social Critic*. New York (King's Crown Press) 1954.

Bateson, F. W. *English Comic Drama, 1700–1750*. Oxford (Clarendon Press) 1929.

Betz, S. A. E. 'The Operatic Criticism of the *Tatler* and *Spectator*', in *Musical Quarterly*, XXXI (1945), pp. 318–30.

Boas, F. S. *An Introduction to Eighteenth-Century Drama, 1700–1780*. Oxford (Clarendon Press) 1953.

Burgess, C. F. (ed.) *The Letters of John Gay*. Oxford (Clarendon Press) 1966.

Clinton-Baddeley, V. C. *The Burlesque Tradition in the English Theatre after 1660*. London (Methuen) 1952.

Forsgren, A. *John Gay, Poet 'of a Lower Order'*. Stockholm (Natur och Kultur) 1964.

Gagey, E. M. *Ballad Opera*. New York (Columbia U.P.) 1937.

Gaye, P. F. *John Gay: His Place in the Eighteenth Century*. London (Collins) 1938.

Herbert, A. P. *Mr. Gay's London*. London (Benn) 1948.

Hughes, L. *A Century of English Farce*. Princeton (Princeton U.P.) 1956.

Irving, W. H. *John Gay's London*. Cambridge, Mass. (Harvard U.P.) 1928.

——. *John Gay, Favorite of the Wits*. Durham, N.C. (Duke U.P.) 1940.

Johnson, S. 'Gay', in *Lives of the English Poets*, ed. G. B. Hill, vol. II, pp. 267–85. Oxford (Clarendon Press) 1905.

Loftis, J. *Comedy and Society from Congreve to Fielding*. Stanford (Stanford U.P.) 1959.

——. *The Politics of Drama in Augustan England*. Oxford (Clarendon Press) 1963.

Melville, L. *Life and Letters of John Gay*. London (O'Connor) 1921.

Nettleton, G. H. *English Drama of the Restoration and Eighteenth Century, 1642–1780*. New York (Macmillan) 1914.

NICOLL, A. *Early Eighteenth Century Drama* (vol. II of *A History of English Drama, 1660–1900*). Third edition; Cambridge (Cambridge U.P.) 1952.

SHERWIN, O. *Mr. Gay: Being a Picture of the Life and Times of the Author of The Beggar's Opera*. New York (Day) 1929.

SIMPSON, C. M. *The British Broadside Ballad and Its Music*. New Brunswick, N.J. (Rutgers U.P.) 1966.

SMITH, D. F. *Plays about the Theatre in England from The Rehearsal in 1671 to the Licensing Act in 1737*. London and New York (Oxford U.P.) 1936.

SPACKS, P. M. *John Gay*. New York (Twayne) 1965.

SUTHERLAND, J. R. 'John Gay', in *Pope and his Contemporaries: Essays Presented to George Sherburn*, ed. J. L. Clifford and L. A. Landa, pp. 201–14. Oxford (Clarendon Press) 1949.

WARNER, O. M. W. *John Gay*. London (Longmans, Green) 1964.

B. THE BEGGAR'S OPERA

1. *Critical*

BERGER, A. V. 'The Beggar's Opera, the Burlesque, and Italian Opera', in *Music and Letters*, XVII (1936), pp. 93–105.

BRONSON, B. H. '*The Beggar's Opera*', in *Studies in the Comic* (University of California Publications in English, VIII, 2), pp. 197–231. Berkeley and Los Angeles 1941. (Reprinted in *Restoration Drama: Modern Essays in Criticism*, ed. J. Loftis, pp. 298–327. New York (Oxford U.P.) 1966.)

BURGESS, C. F. 'The Genesis of *The Beggar's Opera*', in *Cithara*, II (1962), pp. 6–12.

——. 'Political Satire: John Gay's *The Beggar's Opera*', in *Midwest Quarterly*, VI (1965), pp. 265–76.

DONALDSON, I. '"A Double Capacity": *The Beggar's Opera*', in *The World Upside-Down: Comedy from Jonson to Fielding*, pp. 159–82. Oxford (Clarendon Press) 1970.

EMPSON, W. '*The Beggar's Opera*', in *Some Versions of Pastoral*, pp. 195–250. London (Chatto and Windus) 1935.

HANDLEY-TAYLOR, G. and BARKER, F. G. *John Gay and the Ballad Opera* (*Ninth Music Book*, ed. M. Hinrichsen). London (Hinrichsen) 1956.

HUNTING, R. S. 'How Much is a Cowcumber Worth?', in *Notes and Queries*, CXCVIII (1953), pp. 28–9.

KERN, J. B. 'A Note on *The Beggar's Opera*', in *Philological Quarterly*, XVII (1938), pp. 411–3.

KIDSON, F. *The Beggar's Opera: Its Predecessors and Successors*. Cambridge (Cambridge U.P.) 1922.

PEARCE, C. E. '*Polly Peachum': Being the Story of Lavinia Fenton and 'The Beggar's Opera'*. London (Paul) 1913.

PRESTON, J. 'The Ironic Mode: A Comparison of *Jonathan Wild* and *The Beggar's Opera*', in *Essays in Criticism*, XVI (1966), pp. 268–80.

REES, J. O. '"A Great Man in Distress": Macheath as Hercules', in *University of Colorado Studies, Series in Language and Literature*, X (1966), pp. 73–7.

SCHULTZ, W. E. *Gay's Beggar's Opera: Its Content, History and Influence*. New Haven (Yale U.P.) 1923.

SHERWIN, J. J. '"The World is Mean and Man Uncouth"', in *Virginia Quarterly Review*, XXXV (1959), pp. 258–70.

SMITH, R. A. 'The "Great Man" Motif in *Jonathan Wild* and *The Beggar's Opera*', in *College Language Association Journal*, II (1958–9), pp. 183–4.

STEVENS, D. H. 'Some Immediate Effects of *The Beggar's Opera*', in *The Manly Anniversary Studies in Language and Literature*, pp. 180–9. Chicago (U. of Chicago P.) 1923.

SUTHERLAND, J. R. 'The Beggar's Opera', in *Times Literary Supplement*, no. 1734 (25 April 1935), p. 272.

SWAEN, A. E. H. 'The Airs and Tunes of John Gay's Beggar's Opera', in *Anglia*, XLIII (1919), pp. 152–90.

2. Bibliographical

GASKELL, P. 'Eighteenth-century Press Numbers', in *The Library* (fifth series), IV (1949–50), pp. 249–61.

KNOTTS, W. E. 'Press Numbers as a Bibliographical Tool: A Study of Gay's *The Beggar's Opera*, 1728', in *Harvard Library Bulletin*, III (1949), pp. 198–212.

ROTHSCHILD, N. M. V. *The Rothschild Library: A Catalogue of the Collection of Eighteenth-Century Printed Books and Manuscripts Formed by Lord Rothschild*, vol. I, p. 228. Cambridge (published privately by Cambridge U.P.) 1954.

TODD, W. B. Review of Knotts's article, in *Philological Quarterly*, XXIX (1950), pp. 238–40.

WISE, T. J. *The Ashley Library: A Catalogue of Printed Books, Manuscripts and Autograph Letters Collected by Thomas James Wise*, vol. II, pp. 139–41. London (published privately) 1922–36.